The Cricklewood Dome

Alan Coren

Robson Books

For Barry Took

This paperback edition published in 1999 by Robson Books, 10 Blenheim Court, Brewery Road, London N7 9NT

First published in Great Britain in 1998 by Robson Books Ltd.

British Library Cataloguing in Publication Data
A catalogue record for this title is available from the British Library

ISBN 1 86105 259 6

Printed and bound in Great Britain by Creative Print and Design Wales, Ebbw Vale

The Cricklewood Dome

By the same author
THE DOG IT WAS THAT DIED
ALL EXCEPT THE BASTARD
THE SANITY INSPECTOR
GOLFING FOR CATS
THE COLLECTED BULLETINS OF IDI AMIN
THE FURTHER BULLETINS OF IDI AMIN
THE LADY FROM STALINGRAD MANSIONS
THE PEANUT PAPERS
THE RHINESTONE AS BIG AS THE RITZ
TISSUES FOR MEN
THE BEST OF ALAN COREN
THE CRICKLEWOOD DIET
BUMF
PRESENT LAUGHTER (Editor)
SOMETHING FOR THE WEEKEND?
BIN ENDS
SEEMS LIKE OLD TIMES
MORE LIKE OLD TIMES
A YEAR IN CRICKLEWOOD
TOUJOURS CRICKLEWOOD?
ALAN COREN'S SUNDAY BEST
ANIMAL PASSIONS (Editor)
A BIT ON THE SIDE

For children
BUFFALO ARTHUR
THE LONE ARTHUR
ARTHUR THE KID
RAILROAD ARTHUR
KLONDIKE ARTHUR
ARTHUR'S LAST STAND
ARTHUR AND THE GREAT DETECTIVE
ARTHUR AND THE BELLYBUTTON DIAMOND
ARTHUR v THE REST
ARTHUR AND THE PURPLE PANIC

Contents

A Head of Time

What a lucky little borough Greenwich is! It is the luckiest borough in the world. That is because it is the most important borough in the world. Nothing can be done anywhere in that world without reference to Greenwich. It is where time begins and ends, and since it is time that begins and ends each and every one of us on this planet – not to say the planet itself – and begins and ends everything we do, it is not difficult to see why Greenwich is so important. It measured all our yesterdays and it will measure all our tomorrows. That is why we are buying it a £1,000,000,000 floodlit dome, commemorating a millennium we would not have known we were approaching if Greenwich had not tipped us the wink. Greenwich doesn't even have to do anything to remain important after the millennium, either; it just has to sit there with an invisible line running through it, timing all the milliennia which lie in store, until time itself runs out.

Cricklewood is nowhere near as lucky. Cricklewood could well be the least important borough in the world. Everything can be done everywhere in that world without reference to Cricklewood. Nothing begins and ends here. The only thing that began here was the little blue bag in crisp packets, but it didn't end here, because it very soon realised it would if it stayed, and escaped to a likelier borough. Nor does Cricklewood have anything running through it, except people who are trying to get somewhere else. That is why nobody is buying it a dome.

So I am donating mine. When I settled in Cricklewood – a quarter-century ago, according to Greenwich – I had a full head of hair. It subsequently scattered itself all over Cricklewood. It ended here. And since the few sparse fronds that remain will almost certainly be gone by the last midnight of 1999, I intend to stand, on the chime, at the corner of Cricklewood Lane and Cricklewood Broadway, the very hub of here, so that this luckless borough does not enter the smart new millennium entirely unrepresented. It would be nice if there were a decent moon. Floodlights might be a bit, I don't know, over the top.

AC

Someone To Watch Over Me

I lay in bed this morning, trying to work out what I needed, and by the time I got up at half-past nine, I had worked out exactly what I needed. I needed somebody to get me up before half-past nine.

Most mornings, I do not even lie there working things out. I just lie there. Every morning, Mr and Mrs Coren wake up at 7.15, one of them goes off to work at 8, and the other one just lies there, because when he goes off to work, he goes off to it in the loft, and since he doesn't have to go at any particular time, he just lies there. After a couple of hours, he plods downstairs and wonders whether to make himself a cooked breakfast. He would like a cooked breakfast, it would do him good, it would set him up for the day, it would send him bounding into the loft, but he cannot be bothered to cook it, so he stares out of the window for an hour wondering whether to go for a walk round the park instead, it would do him good, it would set him up for the day, it would send him bounding into the loft. But he lives a mile from the park, if he walked to it he would not have the energy left to walk round it; he would have to drive to it, but if he drove to it he would have to leave his car outside it, and when he got back he would find a ticket under his wiper, and a clamp on his wheel, and a gap where his radio used to be.

But if he had someone to get him out of bed at 8.30, the someone could not only make him a cooked breakfast, porridge, boiled eggs, soldiers, but also drive him to the park, wait, and after his walk tell him it was now time to be a good boy and go to the loft and get on with his work.

Yes, that is what I finally worked out this morning. I need a nanny. A nanny is the only cure not merely for the indolence of the solitary hack, but for the habits even worse than indolence which indolence generates. Like smoking too much. I cannot cut down alone, I need someone to cry: 'Take that filthy thing out of your mouth!' Like drinking too much. I cannot cut down alone, I need someone with the sideboard-key in her pinny and a tablespoon in her hand, who, once a day, would poke a small Glenlivet into my mouth. Unless, that is, she had caught me watching television too much: I cannot cut down alone, I have a set in the loft, I watch *Neighbours*, I watch *Countdown*, I watch *Sesame Street*, I need someone to cry: 'Just half an hour a day, my little man, or it's no whisky for you!'

Also: 'Time for your 40 winks!' I need someone to cry that, too. Most afternoons, I rack up 500 winks, minimum, cheek on the desk, knuckles on the floor (especially after four fingers of Scotch and a large *Blue Peter*), but I cannot cut down alone. I need someone to bound into the loft, preferably with a glass of Tizer and a couple of HobNobs, and shake me, and tell me to sit up straight, because it is time to get back to work. And I would not complain about that work, I would not swear or kick the computer or decide to chuck it all in and retrain as a rag-and-bone man, because, if I did, Nanny would wash my mouth out with Lifebuoy and make me stand in the corner until it was time for my bath.

I really need someone at bathtime. I need someone to bath me, and make me all nice before Mrs Coren gets home. If I bath myself, the odds are that when Mrs Coren gets home, she will find me, thanks to the empty glass on the floor, having 500 winks in it, prune-shrivelled, surrounded by bobbing dog-ends, chill to the touch, and thus as far from all nice as it is possible to get. How much more pleasing for Mrs Coren to turn her key in the lock and hear the cry: 'He's all ready, Madame!' and see me tripping down the stairs, ears spotless, hair brushed, teeth flossed, and – because I have been such a good boy – allowed to play with her until it was time to go to bed, or even vice-versa.

Leaving only the matter of catching up on my reading. I do not do enough, it is tricky holding a big book when you are also holding a big glass and a big cigar, two pages and I throw in the towel, what joy to be tucked in by a qualified tucker who would then lilt a chapter or two of Rushdie until my lids drooped Nodwards. Having to knock off a preliminary vesper is a small price to pay.

God bless Nanny, I know that's right. Time to put an ad in *The Lady*.

Adventures In The Skin Trade

I have ten dozen dead weasels in the boot of my car, and I cannot get rid of them. Nobody wants them. At any price. Even free. Now it may be that you will – not unreasonably

– ask why anybody would, there are no weasel recipes, nor do weasels have lucky feet, and you would be absolutely right if this were a simple matter of meat or paws, but it is not. As a matter of fact, these ten dozen weasels have neither meat nor paws, and that is exactly why they ought to be wanted, because the meat and paws were removed for a purpose. The purpose was to leave just pelts, so that these could be stitched together to form the luxurious item I have in the boot of my car. Yes, it is an ermine coat, once worth perhaps £3,000 of anybody's money, but now, it would seem, worth nothing of nobody's.

Which is very sad for my wife's old auntie; or at least it would be if she were not also a late auntie. For when she was still merely old, she bequeathed the coat to my wife, which meant that when she recently graduated to late, my wife inherited it. This was, in its turn, very sad for my wife, because while other relatives came in for elegant inlaid sideboards, nice little watercolours, highly collectable examples of old porcelain and other gee-gaws to be displayed for the delight of all, my wife inherited something to be displayed only if you wanted that same all to stone you in the street. The old auntie did not, of course have this in mind when she made her will, she was deeply fond of her niece, it is simply that she was a trifle out of touch with the moral niceties of the times into which she had survived. To her, rodent rights were a closed book. My wife, who would not, irrespective of current rectitudes, be caught dead in dead weasels, having so comprehensive a phobia about anything between a shrew and a coypu as to send her shrieking from the room if even Tom & Jerry scuttle on-screen, decided to sell the coat.

So I began ringing round the beleaguered rump of furriers who still dare to put their names and addresses into the Yellow Pages, and discovered that they never buy anything

4

secondhand because they hardly ever sell anything first-hand any more. I might, a few suggested, try my local paper, provided I had the sense to offer only a box number rather than specify the whereabouts of an inflammable house, so I phoned the *Hampstead & Highgate Express*; which, after it had had a glass of water and a bit of a lie down, said that it would not advertise fur unless I could come up with wording which showed I disapproved of it. Sensing this to be a less than foolproof sales pitch, I rang off again so that I could call five local newsagents, four of whom declined on the grounds that if they put a card for a fur coat in the window, the window would go before the coat did, and the fifth of whom inquired whether it was code for some special service, girl in a fur coat, man in a fur coat, catch my drift, and when I said no, it was just a fur coat, the moralist banged the receiver down.

Which was when my wife said, oh what the hell, let's give it to Oxfam, they'll probably be able to get a couple of hundred quid for it, the old lady would go along with that, so I threw the coat in the boot – rather than put it on the back seat in full view of any passing weasel rager – and drove round to the Hampstead Oxfam shop.

That is why the coat is still in the boot. Our policy is not to accept fur coats for resale, said Oxfam, once it had finished reeling. These are dead weasels, I replied, would it not be a caring move all round if we saw to it that they had not died in vain? We are not looking at a coat here, I continued, we are looking at a truckload of schoolbooks, an irrigation system, possibly a ton or two of penicillin, when did a weasel last get an opportunity to perform a charitable act like that? She was, I'm sorry to say, steadfast. Sorry not only for Rwanda or Bangladesh, but also for myself, stuck as I am with an item I cannot even bin, lest the dustmen refuse my refuse on weaselitarian grounds. All I can do is bung the

5

coat in the loft and leave it to its inevitable doom. If nothing else, that should please the Moth Rights lobby.

Cereal Killer

It is a big day when a cliché is rewritten. It means not only that an apparently fundamental truth has been freshly perceived, but also that the world which had hitherto held that truth to be self-evident has itself been forever altered. That is why Tuesday was a very big day indeed. Up until Tuesday, we were all content to define courage as grace under pressure. Henceforth, we must all define it as Hillary under pressure. Because on Tuesday, Mrs Clinton had 125 people to breakfast.

I was not, of course, present: I am neither a top catwalk queen nor a reflexologist of the first water, my name is not a household word where international toiletries barons or bullion buffs forgather, the only newspapers I own are stored against the cat's incontinence. But an imagination requires no embossed stiffie to flash at Marine Corps bouncers, an imagination can get in anywhere. That is why mine now yields to none in its boundless admiration for the First Lady's social bottle. For while dinner for 125 may be an elegant delight and luncheon for 125 a rollicking gas, what can breakfast for 125 be but an absolute nightmare? We all know breakfast.

It is the enormous East Scullery of the White House, and the world's leading newly woken are shufffling in, struggling to focus gummy eyes upon their placements before slumping at a dozen Formica-topped tables, each with a leg wonky enough to ensure the spillage of any crockery placed upon it. Many of these dawn invitees are yawning, some are scratching, several are coughing or bugling their noses into wrinkled hankies, a few are examining sleep-crust between thumb and forefinger, one or two are attempting to remove from their footwear the fragments of dogfood that the Clinton pets have scattered about the linoleum, and the rest are staring blearily at the newspapers propped against their ketchup bottles.

There is precious little conversation: from time to time, an extract of this news story or that is read out ineptly through a mouthful of Coco Pops, or a senior senator exchanges the previous night's prostate anecdotes with the ancient banker beside him, or a bestselling moral philosopher begins to describe to the major fashion editor opposite this funny dream he had where he was standing in a bucket and holding a hedgehog but loses the plot when she asks him if he can see any organic marmalade anywhere, or a distinguished Emeritus Professor of Aromatherapy passes his boiled egg across to a *jolie laide* Oscar nominee to ask if it smells funny to her, or a billionaire civil-rights lawyer launches into a long explanation about his shirtsleeve being wet as the result of his cufflink having rolled under the bidet, to say nothing of his having banged his head on the washbasin when he stood up, which accounts for the Band-Aid on his ear, does anyone else have those days when you know you should have stayed in bed, ha-ha, or a Supreme Court justice launches into an insensate outburst concerning the fact that he has just spent 20 minutes assembling the plastic Smurf that fell out of his cereal packet only to find that its left leg is missing – but do not look, at 7.30am, for the authoritative gossip, the unique insight, the brilliant *aperçu*, the immemorial epigram, the uproarious joke that could accompany 125 lunchtime crayfish or 125 evening grouse, for breakfast brains are never in shape to marshal such complexities, even if breakfast tongues were not too furry to articulate them. It is all they can do, when their minions gallop round to the White House with their mail, to cry 'Will you look at this bloody phone bill!' or 'Who do we know in Pangbourne?' or instigate a really interesting debate on the proposition that it is about time something was done about all this junk mail.

But, oh say, notwithstanding the total unpropitiousness of the hour, what else can you see by the dawn's early light? Yes, of course, flitting with relentless charm between the tables, greeting here, chatting there, the new sun winking alike on the matchless orthodontics of the world's most ambitious smile and the brass neck required to keep it smiling, it is the woman who could have us all for breakfast.

Living Wage

After my recent sour lucubrations anent sly insurance companies, I am truly delighted, this morning, to put on record my indebtedness to Legal & General. Without them, I should have had no idea of my family's indebtedness to me. My family owes me £2,104 for last week alone.

I have been able to arrive at this precise figure thanks to the precise figures totted up in L & G's recent report, *Value of a Mum*, in which the unpaid work done by housewomen – childminding, cleaning, shopping, cooking, and so on – was valued at £313 per week. Peanuts. For, when I laid L & G's pecuniary template over my own domestic services, I discovered myself to be worth very nearly seven women. Let us, therefore, open the even more recent report, *Value of a Dad*.

Last Monday, a cadet member of the family, on a flying visit to mix itself a gin and tonic, shut the outer freezer door without shutting the inner flap over the ice-compartment. This caused it to snap off. When I rang Bosch, Bosch said it would come from Hayes and fix it, for £83.99. The £3.99 was for the flap. Flap-fixers were £80 an hour. I left for Hayes. Hayes is not easy to find. It takes £160 to find Hayes. After you have found Hayes, it takes another £80 to find Bosch and give them £3.99 for a flap which you have to take back to Cricklewood in order to find out that it is for a different model, and will have to be replaced at Hayes, which, fortunately, is now only £80 away because you are getting used to finding it. By Monday night, the flap was back on, for only £483.99. Monday night, however, was not yet over, because Monday night was when we wanted to watch a film I had taped the night before, but when I set the VCR in motion, the VCR made a funny little rattle, so we went to bed.

Up betimes on Tuesday to ring Granada TV's service department, to learn that they could not come out before Wednesday but since I am a dab hand at funny little rattles – only last week, rather than throw away £40 per hour of a trained motor-mechanic's time to sort out my wife's exhaust-pipe, I crawled under her car to secure it with piano wire in hardly more than £100, so that it could fall off the next day and enable her to enjoy the diverting badinage of a trained motor-mechanic who swore he thought a low-flying Tornado was driving into his garage – I soon set about dismantling the VCR myself, at about £200, to find out why it was rattling. We were thus able to watch the film on Friday, because that was the earliest Granada could come out, after I rang them on Wednesday.

I don't know how I found time to ring them on Wednesday, mind, given the fact that the mower had to have its annual strip-down and clean for the winter, for which you could be charged £50 by a professional taking an hour to do it, say £300 by an amateur, to include £75 combing the shrubbery for one of those titchy carburettor springs that fly out as soon as you even look at them and cost £100.69 from Qualcast dealers an hour's drive from Cricklewood. But Thursday was a lot better, Thursday went very smoothly, I could have sent in a bill for £650 on Thursday night, you would not believe what a plumber would charge just for clearing out a garage to find his rods so that he could ream a drain which would turn out to be not responsible for causing blockage to a waste-disposal which, even when removed with a King Dick wrench expressly bought for the purpose from a distant builder's merchant which shuts for lunch, refused either to give up its secrets or go back on again without leaking through the rubber sealing-ring which, for some unfathomable reason, is designed to shred if inadvertently over-tightened with a King Dick wrench.

I'd rather not tell you about Friday, which would of course be pay-day if anybody was paying anything, except to say that, according to *Value of a Dad*, my notional brown envelope deserved to contain a further £370: you know what a glazier would charge to repair a garage window that has had a plumber's rod through it, especially when the first pane of glass he brings back from the cutter turns out to be 4mm wider than the frame, and the second one 4mm longer. I tell you, a man's work is never done. Never paid for, either.

Sweet Smell of Success

The moving finger writes; and, having writ, moves on. Which is to say that had that resonant line been writ today, and had its encompassing poem been as successful as it was yesterday, then Edward Fitzgerald's finger would immediately have moved on to nationwide chains of Khayyam Kutprice Karpet warehouses, Khayyam Kosy Karavanserai motels, and Khayyam InKar Kwiksnax outlets, where the peckish driver could enjoy a drive-in flask of wine and loaf of bread without even getting out from behind the wheel.

For literature itself has moved on, and if, in 1998, a book is to be worth writing, it has to end up as far more than a mere half-pound of assorted syllables gummed down one edge. It has to be the fulcrum of a hundred lucrative spin-offs, and not simply films or television series or Lloyd Webber musicals and their Original Cast Albums either, it has to do everything it commercially can, from launching itself at Christmas as a hilarious board game for funlovers from nine to ninety, to endorsing a fabulous range of pret-à-porter cocktail frocks for the fashionable bibliophile. These days, when we literary theorists speak of a core text, we mean that dull little oblong thing which sets the whole glittering ball rolling.

Our scene now shifts, as the more pulse-fingering booklovers among you may already have guessed, to Provence. Well, to a sort of Provence: the sort of Provence where a major typist can sit in the sun, drink in, along with a chilled bottle or three of Bandol blanc, the wondrous world about him – its skies, its hills, its fields, its rivers, its villages, its incomparable flora and fauna, its myriad people – reflect deeply for a couple of moments, and then, dropping his eyes to his lap-top, begin banging out a book which bears hardly any resemblance at all to the reality he has just been observing, in order to commend itself to four million paying customers who require only that their fantasies be vindicated. This accomplished, and the result faxed to his publishers, the typist has only to sit back again and wait for the lucrative offs to start spinning, from sitcoms and pinnies to Weekend Provençal Breaks (in association with Another Newspaper). and Dream Provençal Cottages To Be Won (in association with Another Newspaper Still).

And now, as we heard yesterday, to a fragrance. For the great French parfumier Fragonard – no relation to the painter as far as I know, but you can't be sure of anything these days, art may be just the same as literature, you can probably buy Van Gogh ear-plugs – has just launched a scent called A Year In Provence, endorsed from New York, where he now shrewdly lives, by Mr Mayle to whom numerous smells were flown for his approval, possibly, I'm only guessing, with a little input from his accountant, too. Niffed, it apparently evokes Provence, and I say OK, fine, goodbye and good luck to it; for I now have other fish to fry.

In order to incorporate them into my own forthcoming perfume. For I, those with uneven piano legs may recall, once wrote book called *A Year in Cricklewood*. It did not, sadly, generate any spin-offs at all: no tabloid offered Weekend Cricklewood Breaks or Dream Cricklewood Cottages, there were no glossy Cricklewood Calendars or Traditional Cricklewood Recipe Cards, no ranges of Authentic Cricklewood Peasant Smocks, no Extra Virgin Cricklewood Olive Oil – nothing but a book in a window waiting stoically to be reduced from £12.95.

I now know where we both went wrong. For while, I have to concede, there might be the odd promotional headache when it comes to pushing Cricklewood cuisine, or Cricklewood couture, or Cricklewood wines, or even romantic holidays on the sunsoaked Cricklewood Riviera, there is no question but that Cricklewood exudes an irresistible fragrance all its own: a subtle blend of cod-batter and diesel, of teeming skip and doggy verge, of squattered walkway and shredded tyre, of sun-dried lager and cloven binliner, of a thousand other more elusive constituents of that peripolitan perfume which few can sniff without the tears coming to their eyes, especially if the wind is blowing off Kilburn.

I shall ring Fragonard forthwith. I may become a literary giant yet.

Your Feet's Too Big

Icannot remember the word for toe. No, no, of course not that word for toe, you can see I have remembered that, what I cannot remember is the French word for toe. I am standing here on the Antibes beach, on my own ten toes, and staring down at them as if, I don't know, the shape of them, the disposition, the way I am wiggling them, will somehow jog the memory. I have even gone so far as to hurtle down the arches of the years to fetch up at a black-board on which Eirlys Thomas, MA (Cardiff) is doing parts of the body. How about that?

I can go back 40 years to dredge up my French teacher's Christian name, her *alma mater*, but not her word for toe. Look, she has drawn a mannikin on the board, and I can see her point to his *genou*, descend her chalk and point to his *pied*, but when her chalk gets to the end of his *pied* – nothing.

You are a caring readership, I know, and you will have become concerned about all this. Has he, you fret, hurt his toe in some way, had a crab on the end of it, trod on some-thing, trod in something, got it sunburnt, found a verruca under it, and does he now need to communicate this to the local emergency services? No (but thank you for asking) it is none of these. This is not about the toes I am standing on, it is about the toes the man over there by the beach-bar is standing on; because while I, as you have heard, am stand-ing on ten, he is standing on 12.

Do not stare at them. That is the mistake I made. I came out of the sea a few minutes ago, and because the sea was the Mediterranean one – do you know the French for drain, by the way? It is *l'égout* – the first thing I did was rush under the beach shower before ten billion bacteria could unpack and go to work. That there was already someone under it did not matter, we are a friendly lot on this beach, not to say so commendably post-sexist that I have often shared a douche with those of a differently topless persuasion, but on this occasion I did not have to be circumspect, even with my eyes. Would that I had: for, as I glanced down, I saw that, beneath me, there were 22 toes, and, God help me, I looked up at him, and then looked down again, and, worst of all, looked down long enough for him to have no doubt at all about what I was now doing. I was counting. Just to make sure. Then I looked up again, and caught his eye – not difficult, it was watching me like a CCTV camera – and he grinned, and shrugged, and, after a moment or two, walked out of the douche and, smoothing his hair back, towards the bar.

After a bit, I walked out of it myself. I wanted a drink, too, but more than that, I wanted to apologise. In truth, I couldn't get a drink without apologising: I could not follow a 12-toed man to a bar when our only previous social contact had been my shameless preoccupation with his pedal quirk.

But the word for toe has gone. I know I had it once, but I do not have it now, and without it, how can I apologise? A general apology will not do, because his natural response will surely be to ask me what I am apologising for, and I am unable to tell him that I am apologising for staring at his toes. That I know the word for feet (see above) does not help: by apologising for staring at his feet, I shall seem to be studiously avoiding mentioning his toes. I cannot, since you ask, just stroll over to the bar, smile, and say nothing. This man knows I am interested in his toes. He may even think I do not want a drink at all, I want only to have another sly shufti at his round dozen.

I know what you're going to suggest. You're going to

suggest that I go up to someone else on the beach and ask them what the word for toe is. Thanks. You realise what that would involve? It would involve pointing at my own toe. And suppose the man at the bar saw me doing that, and talking, and then, as one does, smiling, laughing even? The only safe course of action would be to get changed, go into town, find a bookshop, look up the word for toe, come back, strip again, and then go up to him. Fine. Even if he had not by then gone, he would no longer be at the bar, I should have to find him wherever he was, leaving him to conclude that I was not merely interested in his bloody toes, I was obsessed by them.

I do not know what to do. This is a tricky situation. Really freaky.

Weekend Brake

Cometh the hour, cometh the man. It must, of course, be the right man at the right hour: had it been, say, the infant Isaac Newton watching his mother's kettle-lid rattling up and down, there is scant chance that his observation would have led to the 8.14 from Orpington; nor may we be any more confident that had a Virginian potato fallen on Walter Raleigh's head, the world would have ended up with gravity rather than chips. For while serendipity has so often demonstrated herself to be the true mother of invention, she has always required an obstetrician who knew what he was about.

How very fortunate, then, that the man who cometh down the M1 at the hour of 8.40am on Monday not only listeneth to the *Today* programme as he cometh, but also, this being the right hour, suddenly findeth himself fancying bacon, eggs, sausages and fried bread, not to say a grilled tomato or three on the side. For convened at the *Today* programme are two earnest spokespersons, one from the RAC and one from the Council for the Protection of Rural England; and what they have convened for is to argue the fraught toss over the RAC's advice to family motorists in this jammed holiday season to avoid taking motorways to their destinations and take rural roads instead. Unsurprisingly, the CPRE lady is deeply agitated by this, and, no less surprisingly, the two factions are still at shrill loggerheads as their listener, ten miles north of London, spots that the sign for Scratchwood Services has a knife and fork on it. So he leaves the motorway, switches off the debate about the preferred course for the inevitable destruction of his heritage, parks in the last of several hundred spaces, and, negotiating the teeming families scuttling to and from all these serried vehicles, takes his arteries into the Welcome Break restaurant for a welcome furring.

And he is just mopping up the last of the cholesterol with the last of the stodge when two children sprint in and begin nagging the life out of the couple at the next table: the little boy wants more money for the amusement arcade, and his older sister wants more money for the shop. The father says no, they have to be on their way, at which the little boy – mark these words, history – cries: 'Why? We like it *here.*'

And do you know what happens next? An apple falls. A

kettle rattles. We like it *here*. Slowly, as in a dream (and why not, for that is what he is suddenly in) the eavesdropper gets up, pays his bill, walks out into that brass August sun which throughout the queendom is blistering down upon a million cars grinding as many suffering families through the suffering landscape to countless suffering holiday destinations, and thinks: why? They like it *here*.

At least, they very soon would, if the dream were realised. For what do the great British majority require for their annual hols? They do not go to Spain for Spain, nor Greece for Greece, let alone Turkey for Turkey. So, suppose Scratchwood Services offered not a mere hundred cots for zonked-out drivers but a thousand well-appointed rooms for fun-seeking holiday-makers, plus a brace of giant swimming pools, a golf course, a casino, a safari park, a boating lake, a go-kart track, six tennis courts, a funfair, bars, ballrooms, shopping malls, and all of this but half an hour from London, what then? And what, the dream continues, of Knutsford Services, as near to Manchester, or Corley Services, as near to Birmingham, or any of umpteen such current blots athwart each British motorway, serving our every conurbation? Suppose all these were gloriously transformed? Not only would no rural blight be involved (the present facilities were, as you know, all built under the caring auspices of the Eyesore Trust) it would be reversed: we should see imported forests, artificial ski-slopes, ersatz waterlands, fresh-populated, what's more, with trekking ponies, ornamental ducks, a wallaby here, a peacock there, farmed trout leaping in the floodlight-dappled fishing-pool, IVF grouse hurtling from prefabricated gorse . . .

While elsewhere, greenly, pleasantly all England would lie protected. I got back in the car, switched on Classic FM, and, would you believe, they were playing William Walton? I tell you, this was a major hour.

Heart Of My Heart

One barren morning, four centuries ago, staring out blankly over what might as well have been Cricklewood for all the good it was doing him, Sir Philip Sidney sat, as countless hacks have ever done, glumly fiddling with his word-processor, unable to get started. That it was the best word-processor on the market – plucked, you may be sure, from a really top goose – made no difference at all, since it could process only if given words to do it with, and words were just what Sir Philip didn't have; so he hunched there, as he morosely tells us, 'Biting my truant pen, beating myself for spite.' But help, this being 1582, was on the way: Calliope, that emergency plumber of the blocked imagination, spotted a client stymied for opening words, and did not mince her own: 'Fool', said my Muse to me, 'look in thy heart and write,' And, in a trice, Sidney was off and running.

And now so am I. Stuck for an entrance into today's big theme, I too have decided to look in my heart and write. Indeed, I am looking in it *as* I write: there it is beside my desk, pumping away for all it's worth, which is rather more than I feared it was worth last week, when the video I am currently watching on my deskside portable was shot. For the heart I am looking in is the radiant star of an angiogram undergone at the Harley Street Clinic to determine whether there was anything wrong with its coronary arteries, and since there wasn't, the clinic not only let me out again, it gave me the film as a going-home present, along with a big bunch of flowers it had thoughtfully put in my room to cheer me up while I lay waiting for the operation: although what they actually did was cheer me down, because, as I waited, I kept imagining how they would look lying on a pine lid.

But now, reprieved, I find myself bang in the middle of today's big theme: for, as you know, at first light on Monday, Health Minister Gerry Malone sprang from his own fretful cot and ran round to the High Court to obtain an injunction banning the sale of a video entitled *Everyday Operations*. An anthology of the best bits, as it were, from 27 surgical procedures, this jolly item was about to be knocked out at £12.99 in video shops throughout the country to punters apparently eager to sit gobbling popcorn while they watched unwitting NHS patients having their iffy constituents poked, sliced, scooped out and bucketed.

Mr Malone thinks this is, quite literally, a bit bloody much, and he is absolutely right. For while it is perfectly understandable that the viewing public would far rather watch a lung being sectioned or a squint realigned than have to sit through *Sister Wendy's Story of Painting* or the 14th repeat of *Dad's Army*, it is manifestly outrageous that this preference should be exploited by a commercial company for fat profits of which the poor suffering stars themselves get not even a sniff. To wait six years to have your NHS hernia stapled is bad enough, without being cheated of your due percentage of the gate. Aneurin Bevan must be turning in his grave.

Which is why Gerry Malone is barking up quite the wrong tree. What he should be calling for is a comprehensive codicil to those consent forms one is required to sign before surgeons are let loose on one's innards: this would set out everything from the patient's cut of his cut's profits to his billing (below the surgeon's, say, but above the theatre sister's) and his rights in the event of a sequel, eg *Hip Replacement II*.

Until the necessary legislation is in place, however, it

would be a great pity if the public's taste, whetted to a scalpel's edge by the current shenanigans, were to remain unsatisfied. Which is why it is so happily fortuitous that I happen to know where I can lay my hands on a little something to tide them over. It is neither very long, nor very dramatic, but it is unquestionably very horrible – this must be the dozenth time I have watched it, and, look, I have broken out in a muck sweat yet again – and an absolute snip at £2.99 for an evening's rental. Especially as, by way of an introductory offer, each subscriber will receive, absolutely free and his to keep, a full-colour Polaroid of what may well turn out to be a major ingrowing toenail.

The Price Of Fame

It was in the summer of 1988 that a jolly red telephone on wheels first hurtled over the brow of a hill, chirruped a clarion call to the nation's householders, and declared that it was about to change the face of home insurance as they knew it.

And so it did. The telephone belonged to Direct Line, which, through the agglomerative dint of canny targeting, leading-edge cybernetics, innovative marketing, overhead cheeseparing, and an appealing in-your-face cheekiness which cocked a well-deserved snook at those smug behemoths of the traditional insurance trade who had always appeared to be in business more for their own protection than for anyone else's, very quickly seduced a substantial number of their customers.

The jolly red telephone did not, however, seduce me. Not through any fault on its part, simply because of my own endemic inertia. I am all for change, but nothing for changing: however little trouble it may be to do it, it is still too much trouble for me. In order to move from the insurance company I had grumbled about for 30 years I should probably have had to make a couple of phone calls, fill in as many as three forms, send a whole fax, all that. I could not, in short, be bothered.

Until last week. Last week, I suddenly became extremely bothered. For last week the renewal of my household policy fell due, and when I saw that I was looking at a due even more fell than the previous year's, I rang up to heckle. I then listened to a well-rehearsed socio-political monologue on the state of crime, Cricklewood, the economy, and much else, and rang off again, thereby freeing my dissatisfied phone to ring, at long last, its jolly red sibling at Direct Line. This was picked up by Sue. Sue was ace. Not only was Sue charm and sympathy itself, Sue had everything at her fingertips: I could hear them clacketing away, stencilling the details of my bits and bobs against her databased profiles as fast as I could issue them, and within seconds of the last bob being filed, Sue said she had a quotation for me. It was the best quotation I had ever heard. It left Oscar Wilde at the post. It was 60 per cent lower than my current one.

And then a dreadful thing happened.

Sue said she just needed to know what I did for a living; and when I told her Sue went: 'Oh, dear.' So I asked her why she went it, and she said: 'Do famous people ever come to your house?' and I said they did a bit, not many, not often, and what this brought was the sort of brief taut silence that follows a pin being removed from a grenade. Until Sue said: 'I'm sorry, but Direct Line cannot insure homes visited by famous people.' Flummoxed, I asked why. It was policy, said Sue. She would not elaborate. All she would do was say goodbye.

The red telephone shot back over its hill, jolly no longer.

Three days on, flummoxed is what I remain. I could understand Direct Line inquiring if arsonists ever visited the house, or kleptomaniacs, or drunks who might knock over a display cabinet, or tall lawyers who might sue over an unlabelled low beam, or incontinent dogs left on a white silk sofa, or victorious rugger teams left anywhere. But what conceivable threat can the merely famous pose to domestic premises? They do not, at least in my experience, nick the cutlery, stub their fags out on the harpsichord, throw Ming at one another, or bite irreparable holes in the Bokhara. Even beyond my experience, I should imagine that the famous are far more wary of being seen as a threat to property than anyone else, given the career risks, in these tabloid days, of ending up infamous as the result.

But there is a less imponderable point to be raised, if Direct Line is to stay in business, and it concerns the exponentially rising celebrity roster. Each passing day, such is the hunger of our swelling newspapers and our burgeoning TV channels for fodder, more and more people are getting more and more famous: the moment cannot be far off when the celebrated outnumber the humble and the unmeek inherit the earth. So, before that moment arrives, the jolly red telephone would be well-advised to change its policy, if it wants to keep issuing anyone else's.

Tall Story

After a moment or two, I became aware that, from his rear-view mirror, the cabbie's eyes were watching me. I smiled. One does.

'I never forget a face,' he said, not turning round.

'I take a lot of cabs,' I said.

'You were at wossname, Lord's,' he said. 'Week or so ago. Test match, right?'

'Yes,' I said. I thought for a bit. 'But I walked. There and back.'

'I didn't mean that,' he said. 'It wasn't the cab where I saw your face. I don't do weekends. Get to my age, narmean?'

'I do indeed,' I said.

'You were on the telly,' he said.

'Really? I didn't know.'

'Not for long. Not more than, what, half a minute, but as I say . . .'

'You never forget a face.'

'Right. You develop it, in this job. Second nature. Anyway, they put the camera on the crowd, like they do, and there you were, talking to Prince Andrew.' He swivelled round, now. 'The Duke of York.'

'Oh, right,' I said. 'Yes, we'd both been invited to someone's box.'

'I guessed it was something like that,' he said. There was a short pause. 'You looked like you were having a fair old chat, am I right?'

'He's not someone you meet every day,' I said.

'Exactly the point I was coming to,' he said. Lights went

red, the diesel throbbed. 'Look, I hope you won't mind me asking . . .'

'We weren't discussing anything personal,' I said, quickly.

'. . . but how tall is he?'

The lights went green.

'He's about two inches taller than I am,' I said.

'And how tall's that?' he inquired. I told him. 'Get off!' he said. He swivelled again. 'That makes me the same height as him. I'd never have believed it. Never.'

'You thought he was, what?' I inquired. 'Shorter? Taller?'

'I thought he was bloody enormous,' he said. 'Six-two, six-three. Just shows you.'

'Is it important? I mean, am I missing something here?'

'Yes and no. One of the reasons I thought he was tall was seeing him standing next to Princess Di one time, some do somewhere, and he was taller than she was, and I'd thought she was six foot, I'd heard it, read it, I dunno. So that makes her a lot shorter, if he's my height. She probably wouldn't have come up further than about my nose.'

'I'm beginning to understand,' I said. 'What you really want to know is how tall the Princess of Wales was.'

'A lot of people do,' he said, a little sharply. 'It's like Paul Newman. You just do. People are interested in famous heights. Ask anyone.'

'I know how tall Paul Newman is,' I said.

'You're kidding!'

'I haven't met him,' I said, 'but Barry Norman interviewed him once, walking, and I know Barry.'

'Tell me,' he said. I told him. 'You're winding me up,' he said.

'Gregory Peck,' I said, 'really is tall. I met him at a Bafta do.'

'I've never thought about Gregory Peck,' he said. 'People don't. Robert Redford, mind, that's a different matter.'

'You know how tall Robert Redford is,' I told him. 'You've seen *Butch Cassidy*, haven't you? You've seen *The Sting?*'

'So?'

'So you know he's about an inch taller than Paul Newman.'

'God Almighty!' he cried. 'You're absolutely right!'

Thankfully, we had reached my house. Had we not, he might have asked me about James Cagney. I know how tall he was from seeing Michael Parkinson get up to shake his hand a few years back, and I know Parky.

In fact, I know a lot of people who have stood next to people whose height is a constant fascination. That is why I have taken care not to tell you how tall I am. I may start up an information service. Internet, Yellow Pages, local paper, all that. There might well be a bob or two in it.

Goose Takes Gander

It would be stretching musicology a bit to describe what Cricklewood has as a dawn chorus. It is more of a dawn busk. Each summer day, just as morning brings an arm back to fling its stone into the Bowl of Light, an ad hoc avian glee club convenes in the sparse urban greenery around my premises and launches into sporadic spasms of whistle and squawk, most of them atonal, and none of them loud enough to disturb even the lightest human sleeper. That I know about our early birds at all is only because I have on occasion been woken by something else, such as a clunking radiator, and caught, above its plangent bong, a beaky descant from beyond the sash.

Until, that is, yesterdawn; when, at 4am, I was torn from sleep by what could only be the blast of a car-horn: doubtless some selfish toad hurtling past and loosing one off to feed his joy upon another's pain. But after I'd fallen back onto the pillow, it honked again, same volume, so it wasn't hurtling past at all, it was standing somewhere and leaving me to lie wondering whether to get up and vent a throatful of spleen upon whoever in the street out front was doing it – impatient eloper, nervous getaway driver, 24-hour hooter mechanic, whatever – until it honked a third time, and I realised it wasn't happening in the street out front at all. It was happening at the rear of the house. There was a car in the back garden. Someone, somehow, must have crashed through the fence, trapping himself behind the wheel, and was now attempting to alert the emergency services by the only means available to him.

And that indeed, after I had creaked up, hobbled through to the back of the house, and peered out, was – thanks to the half-darkness and the sleep-gummed eye – what I very nearly saw. There was an object on the lawn which might well have been some small foreign job, except that where its wheels should have been were – I could just make out – two webbed feet. A small experimental foreign job, perhaps? A little amphibious Japanese number, being secretly tested under cover of British night? But, as I watched, the vehicle uncoiled its neck, threw back its head, and honked again.

It is somewhat unsettling not only to find an enormous

goose on your darkling lawn, but to find it honking; because at 4am the only thing you can remember about honking geese is that they alerted Rome to invading Gauls, and though you do not, even half-awake, immediately conclude that a raiding party of vengeful French cattlemen is about to sack Cricklewood and make off with its women, you nonetheless cannot help wondering whether some more conventional scallywag might not have breached your defences and even now be going through your spoons.

Downstairs, however, I found all secure. So I went out into the garden to tell the dawn soloist to put a sock in it because some of us were trying to get some sleep. But when I approached, waving my arms, instead of retreating, waving its wings, the goose began waddling towards me, giving off a low staccato warbling, as if accompanying itself on a muted bugle. Now, if one of the things you can't remember about geese at 4am is whether they can break a man's arm with a flick of a wing, or is that swans, you back off; and when I did, the goose lurched past me, hopped up the step and went into the kitchen.

I did not want a goose in my kitchen. Then again, I did not want my arm in plaster. So I did what any coward would do: I made a deal. I took a slice of bread from the fridge, waggled it at the goose, and went back into the garden. Whither it followed me and, passing up the opportunity to break my arm, plucked the slice deftly from my hand, and ate it. And guess what it did then? It put its head on my knee, and let out a low, singularly gentle, honk. I did not know what this meant, I do not have fluent Goose, but I have to tell you that, as experiences go, it was a bit special. So special indeed, that 1 rather believe it has changed my life.

Which is why I have told you this tiny tale: because what

we weekly share, you and I, is me, and if my life is changed, you have the right to know. And what you should know today is that I shall never eat *pâté de foie gras* again. Especially not to the sound of trumpets.

Food For Thought

I really hate things that happened half a million years ago. There are so few of them. Or rather, there are so few of them that we know about. The result is that we can easily go crazy speculating about half-million-year-old things we don't know about, based on the few things we do know about.

I have not slept properly since Friday. On Friday, I learnt that, half a million years ago, Boxgrove Man lost a tooth. Until Friday, I knew only that Boxgrove Man had lost a shin. Archaeologists found the shin a year ago. It was surrounded by a lot of rhino bones, following which discovery I was left speculating as to whether the rhinos had eaten the rest of Boxgrove Man, or whether Boxgrove Man had eaten the rest of the rhinos. The archaeologists did not seem prepared to say, until, a little later, unable to leave well enough alone, they discovered a large number of stone axes, from which they risked deducing that these were used by Boxgrove Man to help him eat the rhinos. They announced: 'The indication is that the site was used half a million years ago for butchering big game.' I could not see why we had to accept this. It seemed to me equally likely that Boxgrove Man had sat there knapping all these axes, possibly with a view to going out and killing rhinos, true, but was taken by surprise when the rhinos snuck up on him. Nor did the fact that so many rhinos died on the site necessarily mean they were butchered there. It is equally possible that eating Boxgrove Man did not agree with them. They might have finished their meal and keeled over. You will argue that rhinos are vegetarian, but they are not vegetarian out of principle: they might have decided to become vegetarian, half a million years ago, after eating Boxgrove Man.

I had only just started sleeping properly again, when the archaeologists issued a further statement saying it was a mystery why Boxgrove Man had made so many axes, but 'it suggests that a group of up to 30 people collaborated in the task of dismembering the carcasses'. Does it? I would suggest that while the concept of Boxgrove Family Butchers is admittedly a possibility, we are in no position, half a million years on, to rule out Boxgrove Bistro. There is no reason, if you accept their original thesis that Boxgrove Man killed Boxgrove Rhino rather than vice-versa, why he should not then have knapped a full canteen of stone cutlery for 30 and set up in the fast-food business.

I lay awake for many a dark hour, thinking about this. If it were so, how did customers pay? Philologists might argue that Boxgrove Diner would not have developed enough language to ask for the bill, but I should counter this by pointing out that few people ever use language for that, they just make a sort of scribbling sign in the air, well within the competence of a race deft enough to knap. Did they, mind, realise that they were expected to pay at all? Might this explain the lone shin? Did the diners, enraged at discovering that they had not in fact been invited round for a free hot rhino dinner plus all the trimmings, fall on Boxgrove Man and tear him limb from limb?

I got back to sleep around early August, and had a pretty good month until last Friday, when Boxgrove Tooth turned up. All the archaeologists got terribly excited, because it had a nasty cavity with bits of food in it, which was why, they said, it fell out. I was going along with that and looking forward to a decent night's kip, when they let slip their belief that Boxgrove Tooth had belonged to Different Boxgrove Man because it was a couple of centuries older than Boxgrove Shin, having been found several feet beneath it.

What makes them so sure? Is it not equally possible that Different Boxgrove Man simply lived downstairs? There is no reason why Boxgrove Bistro should not have been on an upper floor. Many restaurants are actually on roofs. For the view. Unless, of course, it was on the ground floor and the bloke with toothache lived in the basement.

Then again, maybe he was just visiting. After only half a million years, it is, in my insomniac opinion, far too early to dismiss the possibility of Boxgrove Dentist.

Flights Of Fancy

What a great pity it is that there is no longer an airport at Cricklewood. Had it not been peremptorily shut down in 1920 after one of its two Handley-Page four-seaters failed on take-off to clear the chimney of Number 6, Basing Hill, thereby notching up the first fatal casualties in civil aviation history, I could have flown into it yesterday afternoon, absolutely free. Mind you, in order to do that, I should have had to have left my car in the preposterously pricey Heathrow car park, something of a false economy, to say nothing of the cost of having to go back to get it after I had landed at Cricklewood, because it was only by having the car there in the first place that I would have been able to fly to Cricklewood free.

Here – hang on, don't rush off, you know my methods, the point is coming – is what happened: yesterday I flew from France into Heathrow, collected my car from the car park, drove out onto the A4, saw my fuel-light flickering, pulled into a Shell station, filled the tank, settled the bill, and was told that this settlement entitled me to 12 free Air Miles. Do you know what 12 Air Miles is? It is the point you have all been waiting for. It is the exact distance between Heathrow and Cricklewood. But for the unfortunate mishap of 1920, I might, yesterday, have driven back from the filling station to the airport, parked the car again, and flown home.

Crazy? Of course. Craziness lies at the very core of the Air Miles concept. One day everyone flying in aeroplanes will be doing it on free Air Miles, and they will all be crazy, because that is what collecting free Air Miles will have done to them. They will be flying just because they have collected enough Air Miles to do it, and they will be flying to places they do not want to go to, because the best free Air Miles deals you get are, of course, to destinations that nobody would fly to unless they were flying there free; and compounding the craziness will be thinking about all the stuff they have left behind at home which they had to buy in order to get the free Air Miles that were being given away with them. You can see the craziness already, in people's eyes, when you ask them why they have bought a gazebo, or an electronic harp, or a course of fencing lessons, and they start wittering on about the free Air Miles they got.

No more conducive to sanity are the Air Miles you didn't seek. I have never sought an Air Mile, but they keep coming, willy-nilly, they come when I pay my BT bill or my American Express account, they come when I buy this or that, when I eat or drink or stay here or there, they come when I send someone a birthday bouquet: a bunch of 30 mixed carnations from Flying Flowers, say, brings you 36 Air Miles, you could fly from Cricklewood to High Wycombe, airports permitting.

Airports permitting is very important. It is part of the craziness. It is the part of the craziness which concerns the decision as to when to cash in your Air Miles. Because I do not seek them, I do not have many, fewer than 300, and when I look at a map I realise how few places have airports I can fly to on a return trip. I do not want to go to Ipswich and back. I wouldn't mind flying to Barrow-in-Furness, never been there, but that is nearly 300 miles one-way, I should have to take up residence there and start buying things I didn't want in order to get home again. So shall I stay in Cricklewood, making thousands of unnecessary BT calls, filling my car with Shell and driving about to use it up, buying Allied Carpets (one mile for every £1 spent) and Amdega conservatories (250 miles for every £1,000), getting injections at British Airways Travel Clinics (one mile per fiver), and sending orchids to everyone I know until I have enough Air Miles to go somewhere really ace?

I may have to. My marriage may depend on it. Because my wife has a NatWest Visa card, buys nothing without it, and has a drawerful of miles. I catch her looking at travel brochures sometimes. She could go to the Bahamas tomorrow, she could be off to Bali on the morning flight, but me? All I could do would be drive her to the airport, fill up on the way back, and get 12 miles closer to Barrow-in-Furness.

Why Do You Dress Me In Borrow'd Robes?

Macbeth does murder sleep. No question. I have lain awake since midnight thinking of nothing else and it is now half-past four. And yes, since you ask, I did hear the owl scream and the crickets cry – either that or it was the cat next door sorting a mouse out and the people across the road winding their marriage up yet again, it is not easy to put your finger on peripheral stuff when you are struggling to direct every knackered brain cell towards a major career move.

For the prospectus from Macbeth plc arrived yesterday morning. From Stratford-upon-Avon. Express. Recorded delivery. Why did it do all this? It did all this because I had snipped and posted a coupon from *The Times* of 8 May, offering me the opportunity to become involved in making the film for which Macbeth plc had been set up by its parent company, Cromwell Productions Ltd.

Now, since the conjunction of 'opportunity' and 'involved' is invariably a synonym for folding money and almost invariably also a synonym for plughole, you may well wonder why so fly a fellow as I should not have left his scissors lying safely on the shelf beside his bargepole, and turned his thoughts to better things; but that is only because you did not read the coupon. True, it invited subscriptions of not less than £500 in the project, but what it offered in return was not just a share in any net profit of the film, repayment of capital with interest, and a ticket for the world première, all of which one would expect, it also offered what one would never expect in a million years, *viz* 'the right to appear as an extra in the film and a listing in the credits'.

A snip, or what? So I snipped. And now the glossy prospectus lies glimmering beside my bed, open at the application form which dangles a stardom requiring only my filling in of my chosen amount and writing the cheque for same.

But for how much? Put another way, stardom as what?

A tree, perhaps? A basic £500 ought to get me the part of a nice big fir, waddling from Birnam Wood to Dunsinane by virtue, you will recall, of the soldier concealed inside it. Not too much acting demanded there, you just wave your twigs about a bit, possibly do the odd wind-whistle or chirrup, I could do that, I can see the reviews now, 'loath as I am to single out anyone from the stunning arboreal ensemble, if Alan Coren's brilliant conifer does not receive, at the very least, a nomination for Best Supporting Tree . . .' Nor, for another tactical grand, say, is it impossible that Macbeth plc would be averse to the minor textual change of 'Till Crickle Wood remove to Dunsinane', bringing a special joy to countless local tradesmen, many with bills outstanding, though the cheques are of course in the post.

Invest a bit more, mind, and I could doubtless get my entire face on screen, not just one eye in a knot-hole. A couple of thousand for an Attendant, perhaps, three for a

Lord, while five should almost certainly entitle me to a further textual tweak, and very nearly a speaking role:

> Duncan: What bloody man is that? Not him, the other one. (*Camera pans from seeping Corporal to Sergeant*) He can report etc.

Then again, there's the Third Murderer slot: it has baffled critics since footnotes began, just the two come on in Act III, Scene i, so where is the missing hitman? I see him up in the gallery, spotlit, after the rest exeunt – call it Scene i(a) – doing an engaging bit of business, honing his dagger, perhaps, twirling his moustache, rolling an eye, licking a lip, cackling, all that; and if, furthermore, he suddenly whipped off his moustache to reveal the Bloody Corporal a split-second before the spotlight snapped off, we could be looking at a brand new subtext more than likely to put deconstructionism right back on its feet, especially if he reappears in Act V as a tree.

They could cost a bob or two, though, three different roles. That is why I lie here at, now, 5.30, fraught with indecision. A bit like Hamlet, really. Particularly if anyone from Hamlet plc is reading this.

Amphibious Warfare

I know what I want my garden to be. I want it to be a bit of a haven. I want it to be a sheltered enclave for a reflective loll, a fragrant sniff, a strolling gin, a sunbathed snooze. In short, I want it, God wot, to be a lovesome alternative to the unlovesome world outside. Not an analogue of it. Not a metaphor for it.

Yet it suddenly stands poised to become not only both of these, but very much more. Any moment now, my garden could turn into a major issue. Next moment, a test case. The moment after that, a landmark decision. For the issue is one which could go all the way, and after it gets there, then go either way; which is to say that, in three moments' time, I could find myself being either frogmarched in manacles down the back stairs of the European Court by Helmut Kohl and Jacques Chirac, or borne in triumph down the front ones by Bill Cash and Teresa Gorman. It all depends on what I do about my tadpoles.

Every spring for the past score or so, I have lowered a big bucket into my garden pond, and scooped out the frogspawn. I do this because the Common Frog, our only native species, is so threatened that before long our only native species will be the Rare Frog, and not long after that the Stuffed Frog, and this must not be allowed to happen. Since, left in a small urban puddle, very few eggs survive the territorial imperative, they need a hand: the hand waits until the bucketed eggs have grown their tails and achieved enough self-fending proportions to offer at least an even break against predators, and then carries the wriggling bucket-folk into the country for wetland release. Yes, since you ask, they are all called Elsa, and no, I cannot be sure they recognise me again, it is hard to tell with frogs.

This spring, however, was different. The spawn turned up all right, but as, last Monday, I lowered the caring bucket into the murk, I noticed something about the adult frogs who broke from weedy cover at the disturbance. They were not the normal khaki but bright green, they were not hump-hipped but sleek, and their eyes did not bear those dark rings which give our only native species the appearance of a frog who has just passed a really rough night. These items were, there was no getting away from it, decidedly Uncommon.

I put the nursery in the garage, and telephoned London Zoo. The news was not good: involuntarily, without debate, referendum, vote, or treaty, my pond had entered Europe. Or rather, Europe had entered my pond. For what was in the bucket in the garage was the offspring of the European Green Frog. There was, said the Zoo, a lot of it about, and what made this news especially not good was that the European Frog was not bent upon establishing a Frog Community of mutual benefit to all members, it was bent upon establishing such hegemony over our only native species as to see it off altogether. The sovereignty of the Common Frog was on the line: *rana Temporaria* was about to live up to its name, ie, die up to it. For what the European Frog likes eating best is Common Frogspawn.

Stone me, I thought, I have hitherto had a lazily open mind on EC matters, but push has come to shove, and what do I do? Accept the Eurofrog? I may not even have the option, it may well have inalienable rights, I have not been through the Maastricht treaty with a fine-toothed comb, there are probably major footnotes about *grenouilles sans frontières* and the entitlement of *Gastfrösche* to muscle in at will, and here I am with not only a pondful of predators whose rights to interlope are protected by the European Court, but also a bucketful of incipient cannibals who if released will treat their nice new habitat as a bistro serving British delicacies, and if not released but flushed away to protect our already threatened natives could bring me up before the Grand Duchy's Eurobeaks on a charge of whatever the Letzerburgesch is for frogslaughter.

I have thought long and hard about this, and there may just be a way out. Which is for me to wait until the tadpoles grow to froghood, kill them, and eat their legs. This may not wholly answer the core issues, but as a gesture of Eurocompromise, it seems to me to stand in the great tradition.

Any Old Iron?

As a cutting-edge media guru on constant alert for new TV formats designed to ensure my never having to do an honest day's work again, I can't tell you how excited I am by what came to me, out of the blue, last Sunday. I was lying on my couch in a vacant and pensive mood composed of two parts Vat 69 to one part Hugh Scully banging on about bun-footed Ming chronometers, when there suddenly flashed upon my inward eye a vision of how not merely to pinch but to double the already remarkable audience of 12 million his show enjoys.

My show will be called *The Non-Antiques Road Show*™. It is based on the premise that while only some people are interested in curious things some people have, everybody is interested in curious things everybody has. Our scene now shifts to the head of a five-mile queue.

Punter: I wondered what this was. It goes thunk-thunk-thunk and lurches round the kitchen.

Expert: How long has it been in your family?

Punter: One year, five days, but it has been doing this only five days.

Expert: What did it do before that?

Punter: It did crockery. We thought it was a dishwasher.

Expert: Close. It is in fact a former dishwasher. It is now a tin box. If you'd just help me lean it over so that we can examine the underside, thanks, do you see that litte tag? It's called a warranty.

Punter: How interesting! What does it do?

Expert: It runs out five days ago. How much did you pay for the piece?

Punter: £395. We love it for itself, of course, but we did sort of wonder what it would fetch if it came up at auction today.

Expert: Nothing. Next!

Punter 2: I was hoping you could identify this.

Expert: I'm not sure I can. I've never seen anything like it. It appears to be a drawer standing on four vertical shelves, topped by a horizontal door bearing a display of assorted knobs. How did you come by it?

Punter 2: I made it from a kit. The box said it was a side-board.

Expert: I see. And you followed the instructions?

Punter 2: Yes. They were in Japanese, but my old man was in Changi so he knew the odd word. By the way, it is one of a pair. The other box said it was a bunk-bed, but it came out the same. Are they collectable?

Expert: Only if you tip the binmen. Next!

Punter 3: I was given this as a wedding present. I don't know what it is, but when you put a slice of bread in it, it turns black and goes bang.

Expert: Fascinating! If I were you I'd insure it to the hilt immediately.

Punter 3: Wow! So it's something of special interest, then?

Expert: Only to lawyers. If a guest tried it and got fused to the National Grid, you could be looking at the wrong end of six figures. Next!

Punter 4: My wife and I just moved house, and we were very excited to find this stuck away in the attic. Can you tell me what it is?

Expert: It is an exercise bicycle.

Punter 4: What is it for?

Expert: It is for sticking away in the attic. Next!

Punter 5: My father was a keen gardener, and built up a huge collection of these items which I have just inherited. What are they?

Expert: They are known to the trade as sprinklers. You attach them to a hose, run into the spray, hit them with a stick so that they turn twice, then you go out and buy some more.

Punter 5: Should I hang on to them?

Expert: Only if you want to be hurled across the lawn. Next!

Punter 6: For years we used this to prop open the back door, never imagining it was worth anything, until a friend said he thought it might be Chinese. Is he right?

Expert: Yes. I'm pretty sure it's a crispy duck from, at a guess, the late 1980s. The boom in takeaway food has brought countless rare artefacts to our attention. I recently saw a slice of deep-dish pizza which had been down the side of a sofa since the Royal Wedding. Next!

I Spy With My Little Eye

It will, I think, be generally accepted that should you fortuitously bump into the Duke of Edinburgh at, say, some charity hop, shout: 'Good God, fancy meeting you here!' turn to your wife, and cry: 'Darling, I don't think you know Reg Grout, assistant manager of the Cleethorpes Hilton,' scant joy would ensue. Nor would matters be any happier if you merely stood there, eyes narrowed, and muttered: 'Don't tell me, it's on the tip of my tongue, I never forget a face, was it the Boys' Brigade?'

Yet it happens all the time. Identification failure is the constant bugbear of social intercourse – and no less grim is its constant threat, that worm in the bud of every pleasurable prospect, that dread, even as you step out for a jolly party, of what you are likely to step into. You will gush at meeting for the first time someone you have frequently met, you will exclaim how wonderful it is to meet again someone you have never met before, you will inquire after the welfare of cremated husbands and of wives who have long since run off with their aromatherapists, you will ask surgeons how things are in the retail fruit business these days, tell fund managers how much you enjoyed their latest novel, and murmur to your host's mother that if she thinks the food is bad, just wait till she tastes the filth he calls wine, ha-ha, haven't I seen you on *Newsnight*, you look so familiar, or was it down Kricklewood Kebabs?

So is there nothing to be done? Are we all doomed to age ever more forgetfully, simultaneously accumulating more people and losing more brain cells until the former outnumber the latter and we daren't go out at all, lest someone ask us who we are and we cannot remember even that?

Well, no, not if the Massachusetts Institute of Technology is to be believed (a provision you should keep in a safe place, given that you may wish to come back to it before we're done) because on Monday that fine academy announced nothing less than a quantum breakthrough in man's eternal quest for something he knows he could put his finger on, if you just gave him a sec.

MIT has invented spectacles that whisper in your ear. They do this because part of their frame contains a micro camera which focuses on the person standing opposite you, matches his or her characteristics to images data-banked in a titchy computer contained in another part of their frame, and, after a bit, murmurs the person's name via a tiny unloudspeaker hidden in the hook that goes over your ear. You think I jest? Here is project director Dr Alex Pentland: 'It is a system of recognising faces, expressions, hand movements etc, which could be described as the perfect solution to social embarrassment.'

Oh, really? I can appreciate that if you tell the computer to watch out for a tall noisy Greek cove who walks with his hands behind his back, it will tell you when to curtsy, but what of the other thousands of faces, expressions, hand movements etc, I have run into in the course of my life? Even if these weren't attached to thousands of names I have already forgotten, how in God's name – if he's the one I'm thinking of, elderly number, long white beard – are all these to be programmed in, now, the second cousins, the former neighbours, the old school chums, the ex-colleagues, that nice couple we met on Rockall in 1971, need I go on, yes I need, I need go on to the end of time, logging the names and characteristics of everyone I have met since the beginning of time.

Have you any idea, Dr Pentland, of the size of spectacles I should require to accommodate these data even if I ever succeeded in storing them, the earpieces would be the size of cricket bats and what would happen when I walked into any social gathering? The social gathering would clock my enormous whispering horn-rims and groan, 'Here's that sad brain-dead jerk who can't remember anything, don't go near him, you'll have to stand there while that thing on his face sorts out who you are from the 34 other blue-eyed left-handed baldies he might have been at school or Tesco's with, it could take all night.'

By the way, doc, I know MIT. I went to a convention there in 1963, and they made us all wear name-tags, something I hadn't seen before. What a great idea, I thought. Simple, I grant you, but the best ones often are.

Post Mortem

Just to the left of where I sit tapping this out, there is a sturdy shelf with my life on it. It has to be sturdy, because my life is contained in ten big box-files each containing, give or take, a thousand pages. These are my letters; and what, of course, concerns me today is the kind of man my son might be playing tennis with after I am dead.

It concerns me because Martin Amis plays tennis with Zachary Leader, a Roehampton academic, and it is to Mr Leader that Martin has entrusted the editorship of his father Kingsley's letters, thereby upsetting Eric Jacobs, Kingsley's drinking companion, who had been led to believe that he was going to be doing the editing. The snag is that he had been led to believe this by Kingsley, who, not being an executor of his estate, was in no position to lead anyone to believe anything, a situation enabling Martin, who is an executor, to prefer his chum to his father's.

Now, it is clearly important who edits posthumous letters, since the selection will determine our perception of the man who wrote them; and, dipping into the big box files, I see that this is far more clearly important in my case than in Kingsley's. For while his letters were sent to top literary bananas like Anthony Powell and Philip Larkin and Evelyn Waugh and – packed with the sort of stuff one expects when like speaks to like and known speaks to known – will doubtless present a consistency of style, attitude, taste, and above all personality, mine do not present anything of the kind. That is because mine were not written to anybody I know. I never write personal letters. When something personal is called for, I call for it: I pick up a phone. What the big box-files contain, therefore, is impersonal stuff that could be expressed only in writing. It is exclusively commercial. That is why I kept copies.

It is also why its editing is so terribly important. Because, on dipping into it, I find that I consist of umpteen different people. Take the long and riveting 1973 correspondence with Granada TV Rental about their inability to sort out a screen inhabited solely by blue flat-headed midgets: this fine epistolary sequence begins in ironic bewilderment, moves on to anger, becomes incensed, then grows chilling with threat, the work of an influential and well-connected bastard whose editors beg for consumer scams, whose lawyers yearn for easy briefs, whose close friends on the Granada Board are coming to dinner that very night.

45

Now set this against the famous 1977 exchange with Lex Volvo over the fact that, despite six visits to their body shop, the tailgate of my estate still flies open on a whim; this shows a very different man, more hurt than angry, caringly distraught, fearful that, at sudden braking, his children will end up whirling in the welkin above the Ml like Tiepolo cherubs, a decent, gentle man unable to believe that his love of Sweden and his deep admiration, as a lifelong socialist, of its reputation for humanitarian concern could so unthinkingly be put at irreparable risk.

Yet how different both these writers seem to be from the wheedling supplicant of the brilliantly inventive Overdraft Letters (1968–85, *passim*), in which a figure emerges of not only great humility but also extraordinary financial probity and wisdom – one who would, I fear, be unrecognisable to the same period's Inland Revenue recipients, confronted by a fiscally incompetent bohemian unable to understand the first thing about where money comes from or where it goes, and is thus constitutionally unable to keep accurate records, whatever those are.

And can either of these be the man whose passionate correspondence with Barnet council down the long arches of the years addresses everything from wonky pavements and duff binmen to underfunded libraries and sandpit dogs' doings? True, that man is also variously angry, caring, threatening, humble, wise, influential, and the rest, but above all he is – it shines through every sentence – a political idealist pledged to that right to vote which put Barnet council where it is today. The problem for those reading his letters is how to reconcile the lifelong Conservative this makes him with the lifelong socialist who finally persuaded Volvo to fit a new tailgate. Which is why, when I am mortally uncoiled, I need a smart editor. Not just anyone for tennis.

Last Gasp

It was the best of times, it was the worst of times. But though the two cities connected in this sorry tale were once again English and French, and while the former still is London, the latter was no longer Paris; it was Nice. And it was precisely what connected them which makes the tale so sorry. What connected them was British Airways. Flying to Nice on New Year's Eve was the best of times; flying back to London three days later was the worst. For 31 December 1996 was the end of an era.

Let us now roll down the arches of the years to the apogee of that era, and peer, through our welling tears, at a full-page colour advertisement from a 1955 *Punch*. It is, after the vogue of the time, not a photograph but a painting, and it presents us with a man and a woman so effulgently handsome, so effortlessly elegant, so patently sophisticated, that beside them Rex Harrison and Margaret Leighton would look like Rab C. Nesbitt and Nora Batty. Fortunately for Rex and Margaret, however, the only person beside them, as they sit, languidly arranged in two pale blue *fauteuils*, is a tall uniformed cove, standing in respectful half-bow, one tanned hand behind his back, offering them something on a silver salver. It is not champagne, because the couple are already holding two golden flutes (the artist, let me say, is a dab hand at titchy bubbles), nor is it slivers of *foie gras*, because a dish of these nestles toothsomely before them on a little table. It is a packet of du Maurier cigarettes.

In which delightful scene two highly significant further details must be noted: the first is that the fawning uniform is that of British European Airways, and the second is that the brace of tickets lying on the table beside the blobs of goose have 'London–Nice' printed on them. Yes, this is an airliner, it is flying to the French Riviera, and its owners are pulling out all the stops to make a couple of smokers happy.

The object of the entire cheesy composition, of course, being to make millions of other smokers happy; they will be made happy by buying du Maurier cigarettes, for in so doing they will confer upon themselves at least a fagsworth or two of the shimmering glamour efflorescing, as dazzlingly as kryptonite, off these airborne paragons. That, at any rate, is what the agency told the gathered manufacturers, at which point all the manufacturers began nodding vigorously, because they too could conceive of no more beguiling an aspiration than winging to Nice beside a fetching partner, poking major liver into their faces, sluicing it down with Dom Perignon, and, of course, topping it off with an easeful drag on their splendid product. They would be Scott and Zelda, Edward and Wallis, for was that not what the dream of Nice was all about?

Oh, it was, and – you guessed? – for the Corens too. Soppily addicted these 30 years to both the selfsame dream and the selfsame stimulants, they have flown down to Nice perhaps a hundred times; not, mind, eating *foie gras*, this having been replaced in Economy by a lino sandwich and a tinned peach, but invariably drinking champagne from tiny bottles and puffing cigarettes from large cartons. And always on BA, the last carrier to permit smoking.

Now do you sense it? The era ending? It is 31 December 1996. and the Corens are yet again dreaming their way down to Nice, fizz bubbling into their mouths, smoke wafting from their nostrils, they are happy bunnies in their tiny blue-fugged warren at the rear – until, as the aircraft turns on its final approach over the diamond-strung Promenade des Anglais and the No Smoking signs wink on, the steward leans over (not so very differently from that other steward, in 1955) and tells them they are part of history. For this is the last smoking flight to Nice that there will ever be. On New Year's Day, BA goes cold turkey.

The Corens had not known this. They are aghast. The steward, a kindly man, sees this, and says: 'Have you thought about nicotine tablets?' A stricken Coren shakes his head, mute; but he is thinking about them now, as he stubs out the last thing he will ever smoke, up here. He is thinking: you cannot chew a Nicorette and drink champagne at the same time. He is thinking: the No Dreaming sign has just winked on.

Rockery Nook

It is time to come clean. It may go well with the jury. If it does not go well with the jury, it may at least go well with the judge, even if I am unlucky enough to get Judge Alexander Morrison – for, despite sending Freda Cunningham down for 27 months on Monday, he does seem to have the odd caring bone in his body, albeit, in this case, for her victims.

This case was all about bones and bodies. It was about the bones and bodies of the deceased clientele of Freda's Pet Care Cemetery in Weston-on-Trent. Over the years, her undeceased clientele had paid £185 a time to have the bodies of their ex-pets buried in smart wooden coffins with all the trimmings, but when these were subsequently exhumed, not only was there not a trimming to be seen, there was not even a coffin, smart or otherwise. Freda had buried the deceased either in binliners, or in nothing at all, though whether she made this distinction from spasmodic twinges of guilt, or even compassion, was not made clear in court. I rather doubt it, since what was made clear was that Freda was a really nasty piece of work, which is why Judge Morrison felt the time was right for her to make a major career move.

He has my wholehearted support – and not just because I may need his, any day now – for hers was a foul deception, and I sincerely hope that none of my readers will feel that anything but justice has been done. What, however, I no less sincerely hope is that they will feel that justice needs equally to be done when, in consequence of my at last unburdening myself today, a panda from the Serious Pet Squad pulls up at my door to haul me before the beak. The justice I want done then is the one that comes tempered with mercy: for while mine was a deception even more duplicit than Freda Cunningham's, foulness, I submit, had no part in it.

I have a pet cemetery, too. It is the rockery at the end of my garden, and during the auld lang syne when my children were small, scarcely a month went by when something wasn't being interred in it. There was a rabbit called Peter, a guinea-pig called Zebadee, two gerbils called Bill and Ben, a hamster called Sebastian, a tortoise called Morris Doris, three successive frogs (possibly two frogs and a toad) all called Freddy, and a large number of goldfish known only to God – you do not sprinkle names on a pondful of goldfish unless you can be pretty sure which is which. And, since you ask, uncertainty was also why the tortoise was called Morris Doris, since we couldn't find anything on it – or, when held up to the light, in it – to allow us to form a conclusion.

And all these beloved little chums were, when their time came, lowered into the rockery with obsequies of which a clog-popped emperor would have been proud. With, I have to say, the exception of Morris Doris, because it was impossible to tell whether or not his/her time had come, he/she being no more easy of interpretation in death than in life: whether what was inside his/her shell was alive we could not say, but as it had remained inside him/her for three weeks, we decided merely to put Morris Doris on the rockery to see what happened. What happened was that after a further month, he/she vanished, though whether own steam was involved or some more sinister agency, we never learnt.

But, and here is the nub, all the rest have vanished, too: though my children have grown up believing their dear ones to be snug in tissue-lined shoebox, biscuit-tin, or, in the case of Sid the newt, fag-packet, they are deceived. Because after we had interred every one of them, I would covertly dig them up again, and re-dispose of them elsewhere.

I see horror darken the jury's eyes; but it was, I swear, for the best. For the earth is skimpy on a rockery, and I did not want some predator, fox, terrier, cat, magpie, to come along, before the funeral baked meats were yet cold, and leave sad scatterings of bits and bobs upon the lawn. And if the Day of Judgment turns out to be more at hand than we think, so that the sudden rockery yawnings bring to my family nothing but grave disappointment, well then, I shall just have to throw myself upon their mercy as I do now on yours.

If I'm there, that is. I may be elsewhere, doing 27 months.

Social Climber

You don't know how lucky I am. I have been up Cézanne's ladder. It has an iffy rung. I do not, however, intend to tell you which one. Not unless we meet, and you say: 'For me, *Hills and Mountains in Provence* has always been the fulcrum of his development. I'm not talking only about the new audacity, I'm talking about that extraordinary palpability in its structure which shows just how far Cézanne had advanced beyond the mirages of impressionism.'

If you say that – certainly if the woman opposite counters with 'Yes, it was once owned by Gauguin, you know, but the point came when Paul could no longer endure what he called the aggression of its solidity' – I shall put down my fork and say, 'I have been up his ladder.'

I can do a full five minutes on Cézanne's ladder. It was a good ladder, honest, coarse-hewed, thick-poled, peg-jointed, no nails, no worm either, a bit of warp of course, after all this time, but no unsettling whip, you could be five metres up that ladder and not know you were on one, provided you remembered the iffy rung, it had this creak. I can't say whether or not it creaked when Cézanne went up it, a century is a long time in laddering. Then again, it might depend on what he was carrying, he was a big man by 1886 and if he had an easel under one arm, possibly a heavy box of painter's bits and bobs under the other, it might even account for the rung becoming iffy in the first place. We cannot know all there is to know about such things, your Johnny Art is a mysterious cove, and while it is diverting to think that my ear might have shared a creak with Cézanne's, I am not jumping to any conclusions.

I rented the ladder in 1986. Not just the ladder, naturally; you do not load your family into a station wagon and drive to Aix-en-Provence for a fortnight up a ladder. I rented a nicely mottled 18th-century house because it had this terrific swimming-pool with the Mont Ste.-Victoire reflected in it, you could float through it on your back, it was the only view of the mountain Cézanne never saw, the pool wasn't built until 1920. Not that I know whether he could swim, I should have to ask the woman opposite, or that bloke at the far end who was banging on about Cézanne's architectural approach to the female buttock a bit back, green underpainting to relate flesh to rock, all that.

It was the elderly *gardien* who told me about Cézanne going up the ladder. His father and grandfather had been *gardiens* before him, and one of his grandfather's duties had been to prop the ladder against the wall so that Cézanne could climb on to the flat roof for an aspect of the mountain unavailable anywhere else. Many a morning, Cézanne would trudge a kilometre up the lane from the Jas de Bouffin, the house he inherited from his father in 1886, climb the ladder and gaze.

I did that, too. Sometimes, I took a bottle up. Between the first glass and the last, the evening mountainflank would change from pink to blue by going through a million colours between which have no names at all.

I did not know then, of course, what a very important thing this was to have done. That was because I did not know that a huge Cézanne retrospective would open at the Tate today and become the most talked-about event in the whole history of talking. I have already been to two dinner parties and a lunch where they talked of little else and the exhibition hadn't even opened; the scalp crawls at the prospect of all the talking which lies ahead, after everyone has seen the thing. And everyone will see the thing. It is the thinking man's *Mousetrap*.

I do not want to hear anybody's opinion about Cézanne's pictures. I never want to hear anybody's opinion about anybody's. Not least because courtesy requires a response, and before I know it I feel my own jaw going up and down, and hear my own mouth trotting out tosh. Which is why, this time, I am one of the lucky ones. For once, I am in a position to counter the, er, mirage of aesthetic criticism with the aggressive solidity of anecdote. I shall tell them about going up his ladder. And if that doesn't make them put a sock in it, I shall do his bucket.

Because there was this old wooden bucket in the wash-house, and the *gardien* said . . .

Up To My Old Game

For those of us who have given our lives to lawn tennis, this is the biggest fortnight any of those lives has ever seen. That is because Wimbledon '97 is as literal a turning-point as any you could shake a racket at: it is the point at which the game of tennis, having gone as far as it can go, has been compelled to start coming back again. Its progress has brought it so close to extinction that regress is now the only way forward.

Which is why the LTA has reintroduced the Old Ball. It has done this because nobody can see the New Ball. All anyone can see is two advertisement hoardings on either side of a net, one crouching and the other leaping into the air, windmilling his racket. They take turns to do this for a few minutes, and then they go away again, leaving spectators to wonder why they spent all night in a wet sleeping-bag before giving £500 to a man with a cauliflower ear. However, now that the Old Ball has come back, travelling some 10 per cent more slowly than the New Ball, there is an outside chance that some spectators, at least, will twig the connection between the advertisements on either side of the net.

And if, next year, the LTA brings back the Old Racket, which is what it is being urged to do, even more people may see the Old Ball. That is because the Old Racket is made from a tree, while the New Racket is made from stuff invented to go to the Moon in. Since you go to the Moon at 25,000 mph, it is easy to see why it is not easy to see anything hit with the New Racket.

More encouraging still is the news that the International Tennis Federation is considering the introduction of both a higher net and a slower playing surface, which, if adopted, will enable almost everyone to fathom the relationship between Old Balls, Old Rackets and advertisement hoardings. And were the happy regression implicit in these four crucial areas to continue, the benefits to tennis would be well-nigh incalculable.

How I can be so confident of all this? I can be so confident of all this because that is exactly the way Cricklewood '95 is played. I have been using the Old Ball since Cricklewood '67, and I am here to tell you that even though age may have withered it a bit, custom has not staled its infinite variety. Though bald, it still bears my initials, so that when, thanks to a combination of its wizened aero-dynamics and one or two other key factors, it strikes the netpost and loops elliptically into the next-door court for identification and retrieval, things happen which are of enormous interest to spectators, particularly if the next-door court is standing at match point. Were this to happen on the Centre Court forcing Ivanisevic, say, to nip next door onto Court Number One for a squint at Henman's ball prior to a punch in the mouth, public interest could rise to unprecedented heights.

As to those whose other key factors, while a higher (in some places) net, and a slower playing surface – thanks to old Perrier bottles rolling around, big daisied cracks, and a certain amount of cats' doings – are not without signifi-cance at Cricklewood '97 in making the Old Ball hop competitively about, the major role unquestionably belongs to the Old Racket. Not only has the original wood been enhanced with Elastoplast so that there is now twice as much rim available for those tricky netpost shots, but the absence of several strings means that should the ball ever fail to meet the rim and instead accidentally strike the racket-face, it could well come off it again at an angle so unfathomable as to send Euclid back to the drawing-board.

Who can doubt that, were such kit to be deployed at Wimbledon, a bracing wind of unpredictability would make such nonsense of the seedings as to restore the tour-nament to the status of the truly Open Championship it currently claims erroneously to be? Whether that would be enough to revive our national tennis fortunes it is of course too early to say, but were the All-England Committee to justify its name by introducing say, the mandatory Open Sandal, the Pre-Match Pork Pie, and the Inter-Set Large Gin, anything is possible.

When Dinosaurs Ruled Cricklewood

The Natural History Museum is not going to like any of this, but it has only itself to blame. Itself and my father. And Jake the Staffordshire bull terrier. Throw in Professor Mark Norell. And Michael Crichton. And Fred Flintstone. But not me. I am blameless.

Let us go back 118,000,000 years, to the Isle of Wight. Or what is now the Isle of Wight. It was not the Isle of Wight then, it was not an isle of anything, it was merely a large hummock from which, if you walked due south, you would wind up in Africa. I say you, but it was not you, of course; you had yet to evolve, walking for you was aeons away, you were not even a twinkle in a mollusc's eye. What was walking across the incipient IoW at that time, possibly bound for Kilimanjaro, possibly just back from it, was a giant iguanodon. We know it was giant, because half its arm was four feet long, and we know that because half its arm has just been dug up by Jake the Staffordshire bull terrier, who found it while out walking with his owner, John the Isle of Wight human being. I do not know the iguanodon's name, but there was a photograph of the three of them – all right, the two-and-a-bit of them – in the papers two days before Christmas, and they all looked pleased with themselves, even the armbone, as well they might.

For they had crowned a major dinosaur year. It was a year in which seriously big bits of dinosaurs had been found everywhere – from half a stegosaurus in Yucatan and most of a diplodocus in Arizona, to, in the Gobi Desert, not merely an entire oviraptor but an entire oviraptor brooding over its entire clutch of eggs, having been poignantly struck in mid-brood by a sudden sandstorm, to the somewhat heartless joy 80 million years later, of Professor Mark Norell of New York, who was thus able to prove all sorts of theories for which he had hitherto lacked, literally, concrete evidence.

He got very excited, which is why I blame him, just as I blame Michael Crichton for the palaeontological mania generated by *Jurassic Park*, Fred Flintstone for coining 'Yabbadabbadoo!' as the only expression adequate to Mesozoic rapture, and the Natural History Museum for pandering to all this frenzied saurophilia with its endless cheesy exhibitions, triceratops T-shirts, toy pterodactyls, Tyrannosaurus rex ice-lollies and ornithischian board games. Thanks to all these, variously worthy or commercial, dinosaurs have been manufactured into a human obsession.

Which brings me to my father. My father had an obsession of his own. He always went out on Boxing Day morning to dig the garden. A spot of digging was, he maintained, the surest way to deal with the excesses of Yuletide indulgence. It cleared the head. It worked off the flab. It opened the pipes. It sorted you out. I don't know whether he believed all that (I never once saw my father hung over), but digging is what he always did, and it has come to be what I always do, because I do believe all that. For I have seen me hung over, and I know for a fact that a spot of digging works wonders, never mind the added value which a vigorous solstice aeration and a sprinkle of permeating mulch confers upon the pre-vernal sod.

So I was out there, yesterday morning, forking the robin-hopping clods and thinking about nothing in particular when something in particular wormed its way, willy-nilly, into my thoughts. I began to think how satisfying it would

be to see off Jake the Staffordshire bull terrier, and crown
the dying year, at the eleventh hour, with some chart-
topping fossils of my own. For Cricklewood, too, was
joined to Cape Town, once: big things lurched here at No
26.

By noon, I had a pile. But how is a layman to know
whether this is a bone that looks like a stone, or only a stone
that looks like a bone? You'd need a dog. Or a Natural
History Museum. I shall be there first thing tomorrow, bin-
bag in hand. It has only itself to blame.

A Lot Of It About

Not so very long ago, when I had this, the course of
action was a doddle. It was a course of inaction. I
stayed in bed, the quack came round – quacks did that then
– told me there was a lot of it about, and went away again.
I took two aspirins in a tumbler of Glenfiddich, pulled the
blankets up to my chin, switched on *Gardeners' Question
Time*, and thought no more about it.

Today, I have got this and I cannot think about anything
else. That is because, today, this could be everything else.
You know what this is, you may indeed very well have it
yourself, this is the one where your throat has rusted, your
brain has swollen up against the inside of your skull, and

your eyes cannot be swivelled without your ears whistling. And when you have this, today, you do not do the nice thing with the blankets and the booze and the radio, you lie staring at the ceiling, rewinding your entire life in the frantic hunt for epidemiological clues.

How many hamburgers have I eaten? How many steaks, chops, stews, bangers, Oxo cubes? Lifetimewise, we could be looking at something in the order of four tons of beef. Should we not therefore be looking at something in the disorder of four tons of beef? The odds on a bit of mad gristle are unnervingly short. There is a lot of it about.

How many eggs, these 50 years past? 25,000? And are we entirely confident that every single one of these slid through my guts without leaving a salmonella bug or two behind, to nestle in the dark, gathering strength, biding its time?

Listeria? Might well have taken on a ton of it by now, variously disguised as cheddar, edam, reblochon, gorgonzola and all the rest, I have travelled the world for half a century gobbling bacteria on biscuits – billions of them washed down, to make diagnosis worse, with plonk contaminated by everything from insecticide and cork-mould to *vendangeur's* widdle and Austrian anti-freeze.

Have I inhaled much lead since birth? Drunk much strontium 90? Ingested many iffy additives, popped many dodgy medications? Were my windows open when Chernobyl went phut? Did I ever live near electricity pylons? I can't remember for the life of me – literally – but that might be one of the symptoms, unless of course it is one of the symptoms generated by sitting in front of a VDU all day, particularly if I did it in premises which could well have been going down with Sick Building Syndrome, a condition very probably complicated by its situation beneath a major ozone hole or above a Victorian sewer, more than likely both. And at a time when there was a lot of Seasonal Affective Disorder about. Compounded by the fact that the air-conditioning had been left on to allow the legionnaires' bacteria to stretch their legs.

What I can remember is umpteen incautious holidays spent swimming in various waters which only a fish would be caught dead in: I have not only breast-stroked the neat mercury off Japan and crawled the Mediterranean Effluent, I have floated on my back to watch the sun go down behind Sizewell-B and paddled the Cornish fore-shore in search of the wherewithal to make luminous *moules marinières*. Can it be long before all these chickens come home to roost, particularly if they have been fed with those hormones which, I have reason to believe, could any minute generate beneath these pyjamas the first tell-tale stirrings of a nice firm bust?

So you will understand that my course of action is rather less of a doddle than heretofore. I lie in my bed, with, I see from my paper, 12 million housemites in the mattress beneath me, God knows where they've been or what they picked up there, and I watch the mysterious specks turning in the afternoon sunbeams, wondering how long it will be before we all begin coming down with Pernicious Mote Syndrome, and I think, should I hobble round to the quack, should I hell, imagine what I could catch off him, never mind the very strong chance, I see from my telly, of my winding up on some clapped-out, under-funded, cross-infected ward with a syringe inside me and the wrong leg cut off.

Fairy Tale

She was born to ding-dong merrily on high. That was her life's work. That was the career her Creator had marked out for her, ten thousand miles from Cricklewood. 'You will be flown to Cricklewood,' he murmured, tenderly but firmly, 'you will be placed on high, and once you are up there, you will ding-dong merrily.'

I may be taking small liberties here, I do not know exactly what he said, I wasn't there, but I feel fairly confident that he said something; you cannot sit all day in the middle of the South China Sea knocking out electronic fairies without the work getting to you a bit, especially as you cannot talk to the assembler next to you, they are strict disciplinarians in Taiwan, turn to your neighbour for a natter and you will be out on your ear. It is therefore not unlikely that you would murmur to the fairy between your fingers, to stop yourself going nuts.

The scene now shifts to Camden Market, last Saturday, whither a man has gone whose old fairy appears to have done a runner; for it is one of the Parkinsonian laws of Christmas that work expands so as to require twice the time available for its completion, make that thrice if the work involves a tree. For example, because you are an old hand at the Yule game, you allow an extra hour for rushing out to buy new lights, only to find that the old lights actually work, for once, so you cry 'Wow! Terrific! I have been granted a whole extra hour to rush out and buy the chocolate Santas I thought we already had!' and then you reach into the lights box to get the fairy to put on the top of the tree, but she has gone, so not only does the whole extra hour go in looking where she isn't, you now have to find three new hours to rush out and buy another fairy.

One of these is spent in not discovering them in any local shop, a second is spent parking just outside Wolverhampton, this being as close as you can to Camden Market on pre-Christmas Saturday, and the third is spent trudging through the stalls until you find the only man who sells fairies. He does not, though, sell fairies like your old fairy, who, Yule in, Yule out, just clung there silently blessing the household with a wonky wand, he sells only fairies who sing *Ding-Dong Merrily On High*. 'They got this chip in,' he explains. 'They wossname every hour, on the hour.'

So I gave him a tenner, and took her home. She said nothing in the car. She said nothing when I put her on the tree. And then, after about ten minutes, she sang 'Ding-dong merrily on high'. After another ten minutes, she was still singing it. I took her down again, and, with this technical expertise I have, shook her. She did not stop. I tapped her lightly against the banister. 'Ding-dong merrily on high!' she sang.

This was bad news. There were 21 days to go until Twelfth Night, and there was quite enough coming up in those 21 days which would threaten to drive us all barking mad, without having an incontinent Chinese soprano to help out.

I took her into the kitchen, put her on the table, and removed her clothes. She had, sorry about this, a little hatch between her legs, which, it would seem, led to her works. So – this is the fourth hour by now, and, if I haven't mentioned it, I had forgotten, while out, to buy the chocolate Santas – I put a screwdriver to the hatch. It was a bit unsettling, performing major abdominal surgery on a patient singing 'Ding-dong merrily on high!' but I persevered, even when I discovered that I could not open the hatch without first prising her legs off. I would have unscrewed them, but they didn't unscrew, they had little rivets. I could now get to her innards. They had a tiny digital-watch battery in them. I took it out. She shut up.

All I had to do now was get her legs back on. I got one leg back on. Ask me where the other little rivet went. Ask me how long I took to look for it. Unsuccessfully. But I put her back on the top of the tree anyway. No one would notice, right up there.

I'd just finished when Mrs Coren came through the front door, lugging shopping bags. 'Why has the fairy got only one leg?' she inquired.

'I bet you forgot to buy chocolate Santas,' I said.

Little Shop Of Horrors

Since I know my readership to be as caring as it is observant, I feel sure you were deeply concerned as to why, in all the charming snaps of yesterday's Harrods book-signing session, there was not one single shot of the Duchess of York's radiant, and celebrated, feet. Well, I have taken up the matter on your behalf and it appears that, on the best medical advice, her ankles were shackled to the table-leg. For had she got loose in the giant store for even a couple of minutes, the sole object of the exercise would have been defeated utterly: instead of signing her way out of debt, the poor soul would have signed herself far deeper into it. Any royalties (if she will pardon the expression) that her auto-graphing managed to accumulate would have been derisory when set against what that same nib could have got up to on a stack of credit-card slips, as bracket clocks, train sets, three-piece suites, onyx chessmen, top hats, boiled lobsters, slide trombones, electric whirlpools, dinner jackets, gazebo kits, cricket stumps, mantel mirrors, pedal bins, mountain bikes, fancy mice and all the rest piled up at customer collection points.

Because, as she has so poignantly revealed, the Duchess suffers from what she has identified as a serious disease. An epidemiologist of considerable, albeit amateur, standing, she has concluded, after years of research, that it's a bit like bulimia, but with more designer labels. Its symptoms are unmistakable. If you catch it, you cannot stop shopping. You buy anything. You buy everything. You go broke.

And even as my heart goes out to her today, my gratitude goes, too. For in bringing into the open a disease which hitherto had dared not speak its name but which now enters the medical canon as High Shopping Pressure, she has enabled me, at last, to see that what I had always believed to be some kind of character deficiency in myself was in fact the symptom of a major illness which is clearly the obverse of her own. Unable to shop, incapable of buying anything, I now realise that what I suffer from is Low Shopping Pressure.

Here I am in Harrods. I have come to buy ties. I have ties at home, bought by other people, but they have grown vari-ously wrinkled, frayed or eggy, and I have been urged to buy new ones. I stand in front of a hundred assorted spots and stripes for half an hour. I pull some out. I knot some on my finger. I take some to the mirror. Then I put them all back, and think: what I really need is socks. I look at a lot of socks. They do not seem very different from the socks I have at home.

After I have picked up a hundred shirts and put them down again, I try on trousers. I keep coming out of the changing room and staring at legs I do not know. As I pull my own trousers back on for the last time, my wallet falls out. I notice how battered it is. I spend half an hour in the wallet department. I know it has been half an hour because I look at my watch. It is not much of a watch. It is less much than my wallet is.

Luckily, the watch department is nearby. It is full of great watches. After a while, however, they do not seem to tell the time any better than mine. Perhaps all mine needs is a new strap. I examine a lot of straps, until it occurs to me that a new strap might make my old watch look even older. Unlike a gold Dunhill cigarette lighter – provided, of course, that I held it in the hand my old watch wasn't on the wrist of.

I have always fancied a gold Dunhill cigarette lighter. I now look at so many of them that I lose track of why I always fancied one. But having driven all the way to Knightsbridge and found a parking space where, thanks to how time flies when you are unable to buy anything, I will now find a £30 ticket, it seems a pity not to get a hat, and brown brogues to go with it; but once it transpires that my illness prevents me from buying the it for them to go with, I find myself walking about in a sequence of silk dressing-gowns which I have always fancied would be just the thing to pull a gold Dunhill out of the pocket of. But not, all things considered, a tin Zippo.

Wouldn't it be better to buy a new tennis-racket? I have heard about these revolutionary big rackets, they can improve your game no end. Oh look, I am walking into the sports department, it has 38 revolutionary big rackets, I am practising my backhand on each of them, oh look, I am walking out of the sports department, how can I know which big new racket will most improve my game no end, and what's wrong with my old little racket, anyway?

What I ought to do is pop across to the book department. The Duchess might still be there. She could buy me things, if I could get her shackles off. Even if I couldn't, she might be able to recommend a good doctor.

The Spy Who Went Out In The Cold

At the height of the Korean War, I was an agent for the Government. It was difficult, dirty, sometimes dangerous work – open only to volunteers – but someone had to do it, and I was proud when, from the handful who had put their names forward, mine was selected. What I had to do, when so commanded, was go into the lavatories, bend down, and look through the gap at the bottom of each cubicle door to see if there was a boy in it. If there was, I would first attempt to identify him from his shoes, but, should that fail, I would stand up tap on the door, and cry: 'Who are you?' Upon receiving the response 'Who wants to know?', I would roundly declare, 'I am the 3a lavatory monitor.' For so I was. I was delegated to look under lavvy doors because boys asking to be excused often did not come back in the time the teacher believed to be required. I was then sent to find out why.

I have not, for various reasons, spoken of this before, and do so now only because these credentials will endorse my entry into the education debate now being so heatedly contested between the two main parties. The Tories, as you know, believe that the multitudinous crises in British schools could all be resolved by the general reintroduction of the Combined Cadet Force, bringing with it not only toecaps children could see their faces in but Lee Enfields with which they could cut down, say, a drug-dealer or inadequate teacher from 400 yards; while new Labour has committed itself, predictably, to the softer but no less inspired solution of putting every pupil into a nice new blazer, cap and tie, all smartly embroidered with the school motto. Each party views its policy as an infallible means not only of instantly reintroducing everything from discipline, *esprit de corps*, personal pride, respect for authority, clean ears and really terrific GCSE results, but also of preparing children for the adult world beyond, especially if they intend going into the SAS, on the one hand, or catwalking, on the other.

However, while there is clearly much to be said for both solutions to the present educational malaise, neither is quite the panacea it purports to be, since each system suffers from an inflexibility likely to exclude many pupils. These schemes are also, given the cost of grenades and worsted, huge potential burdens on the taxpayer. Allow me, therefore, to advance a third policy with the benefits of both and the demerits of neither. It is the reintroduction of the school monitor.

Let us go back to 1952. To what has been called the

Golden Age of Monitoring. There were blackboard monitors, prepared, for the sake of others, to spend their days looking like little old flour millers, and inkwell monitors likewise prepared to face the wrath of mothers who had sent them off in white and got them back in blue, there were milk monitors, as adroit of crate, quick of straw, and vigorous of mop as they were alert to the countless wiles of the lactophile, window monitors whose deft poles no jammed transom could long withstand, dinner-queue monitors able to keep 500 jabbering gluttons in lines that would put Grand National starters to shame, there were break monitors and kit monitors and book monitors and bell monitors and . . .

And now there are no monitors. A system which, at no cost whatever, taught service, order, discipline, leadership, responsibility, social and communication skills, to say nothing of countless practical techniques which would be of incalculable value in later life, has gone forever. My research among teaching friends brought only shrieks of terror at the very thought: did I have any idea of the potential ructions attendant upon subjecting a child to ignominious manual labour, chalk dust in the lungs, window pole poking someone's eye out, bell falling on foot, did I realise that a cubicled pupil who had had his shoes looked at would, at the end of months of expensive counselling, unquestionably be entitled to several thousand pounds in compensation?

But all that is precisely the situation we have to change, if we want not only exam results to equal any in the EU but also a citizenship of quality. Ask anyone who knows me, and they will unhesitatingly attest that looking under lavatory doors made me the man I am today.

Eating Like A Bird

Much as I hate the thought of any of my dear readers, even before this paragraph has trundled to its close, crying 'Right, that's it then!' and turning irritably to the crossword, I no less hate the thought of wasting their precious time. I therefore feel caring-bound to say that if you are someone who thinks that there is quite enough to worry about as it is, today's cobbling is not for you. Racked as you already are by agonies over monetary union, ozone holes, NHS underfunding, mislaid Ukrainian warheads, environmental pollution, prison policy, collision-course asteroids, Chinese ambitions, greenbelt despoliation, royal yachts, mad cows, blazing Chunnels, millennial profligacy, Internetted smut, nursery vouchers, drug abuse, privacy invasion, and the 89 diseases from which you began suffering the instant Dr Stuttaford finished describing their symptoms, I urge you to seek a safer haven than this. You do not want to hear what follows.

At a little before noon yesterday, having spent several hours in the attic groping for syllables, I threw open the window to expel the thick blue smoke of an emptied pack – neighbours of the disposition of those readers now no longer with us will immediately have slammed theirs shut in terror – and went downstairs to make a sandwich. It was a good sandwich, fresh crusty wholemeal bread, thickly buttered, embracing several slices of best Scotch smoked salmon, and about to be made even better by the large glass of Meursault now being brought upstairs with it. Since, however, it could be made better yet by the wedge of lemon I had forgotten to bring, I put the plate on my desk, and ran downstairs again.

When I returned to the attic, it was immediately borne in upon me that the sandwich might, in my absence, have become not quite as good as it had been when I left. That is because there was a pigeon standing on it. It did not stand there long, choosing instead to take off again through the accessing window at a speed and trajectory which would have left its clay cousin at the post, but what I did not know was how long it had been standing on my sandwich before I had come back. I had been away for perhaps a minute, and while it was possible that the pigeon had flown in and landed only a second before I returned, it was equally possible that it had been there for the full 60. It might, in short, have had the time not just to stand on the sandwich, but to walk about on it. Or round it, pecking as it went. It was important for me to know these things, for while I am not – unlike the dear readers no longer with us – a person to worry unduly about the risk of a pigeon's footstep, the thought that the bird's beak might have had a go at my lunch, drilling into it with a beak recently used for dismembering worms, was a different matter.

I examined the sandwich for beak-holes. I even took a magnifying-glass to it. However, since wholemeal bread has, as you know, an open weave, in order to determine whether the dozens of little holes in it were made by a pigeon or merely by a baker, you would have to know the diameter of a pigeon's beak. Odd, how a man can get to my age and not know something like that. The only option was to lift the bread and see whether there was a hole in the salmon. There was not. But as I closed the sandwich again, raised it, and prepared to bite into it, I suddenly wondered whether I might have been unwisely blasé about the footstep.

I put the sandwich down again, and rang the Royal Society for the Protection of Birds. It would have been more

71

logical, of course, to ring the Royal Society for the Protection of Humans, but it wasn't listed. Was there, I inquired, any disease that a man could catch off a pigeon?

You know the answer. Would I have warned off all those dear readers, otherwise? The answer is that there is almost no disease that a man cannot catch off a pigeon, there is pigeon-fanciers' lung, there is pigeon-mite dermatitis, there is ornithosis, chlamydia, iritis, salmonella . . .

I threw the sandwich in the bin, thinking: is there anything anywhere which is not out to get us, given half a chance? If it ever emerges that crosswords cause brain damage, the responsibility could kill me.

Not To Be Sniffed At

Were you, on the off-chance, to inquire why I was so grateful today to Mr Chandler Thomson and Ms Alice Dale, commodity traders of New York City, I should reply that it was because it's been far too long since I last gave serious consideration to the legs which so signally interfered with my ambition to be a dab hand at *Beowulf*. Chandler and Alice have, though they do not know it, jogged the memory of 40 years: in a trice, they have borne me back not merely to the reading room of the Bodleian Library, but to the very shaft of moted sunshine in which, that distant spring, I sat, the great epic open on the desk before me, my Anglo-Saxon dictionary to the left of it, my notebook to the right, my eyes down, my nib poised – and my ear cocked for the next mind-blowing susurration as the stockings opposite slowly crossed one another yet again.

Where the mind was blown to need not be specified; what was more important for me then, as it is for Chandler and Alice now, is where it was blown from. Driven off-course, day after day, by the siren chorus of a dozen under-graduttc thighs, it left the books, it left the desk, it left the room, and by the time it had struggled back, it was in no shape adequately to deal with yogh and thorn. Most mornings, indeed, it had to be taken outside, leaned against a wall, and given a recuperative fag. That is why I never became a dab hand at *Beowulf*.

Not, of course, that Chandler and Alice are required to concentrate on Old English lettering. Old English letters are not commodities: had you, in 904, put all your money into yoghs and thorns, you would be broke today. What Chandler and Alice are required to concentrate on is sugar and spice and all things volatile: they sit with their eyes glued to their screens, and when they see the spot price for faggot futures go from 17.2 points to 17.4, they make themselves and their clients rich; but if for any reason their eyes become momentarily unglued, and faggot futures drop back down again to 17.1 without Chandler or Alice clocking it, they and their clients could well wind up squatting in Wall Street with a tin cup and a banjo.

That is why the pair, as you may have read, are currently locked in furious (and, this being New York, litigious) battle over Alice's scent. For Chandler's trading performance had been falling off for some weeks, and when his superiors voiced their concern, Chandler was politically uncircum-spect enough to blame this on his having been distracted by everything from the Chanel No 5 with which Alice, who perched beside him, sloshed on each morning, to the various areas whereon she sloshed it, many of which were covered in little else. Hearing this, the superiors, being more feministically illiterate even than Chandler, politely invited Alice to dress down a bit, and give a shorter tweak to the perfume pump.

Alice of course, went nuclear; tactically nuclear, I dare say, or, on second thoughts, don't dare. Pausing only to observe that a big reason for her own performance's outshining Chandler's was 'because I feel good in my body', she Porsched round to her lawyers, who are now seeking a public apology from both Chandler and the firm, plus a million bucksworth of emollient. Fine, par for the US legal course, nothing to write home or columns about, but wait, who is this in the screaming Ferrari only two blocks behind Alice? Yes, it is Chandler, on his way to instruct *his* lawyers to counter-sue her for 'ambient harassment', worth, this time, two million dollars. Now, this one is not par for the course at all. This one is several strokes under, each of which, I have no doubt, America's lawyers will henceforth be straining to pull. Might this doctor have developed a career-threatening tic as the result of his patient's cleavage, did the woman sitting opposite that top novelist on the subway wink at him, thereby wiping the plot of his next bestseller forever from his brain, has this billionaire lost count of his money after the brushing of his knee by one attached to a voluptuous dinner guest?

More to the point, when we, as we invariably do, follow where the US has led, might I be able to track down the owners of those stockings without which I could well, today, have been a Regius professor?

Mulch Ado

I am given to understand that you have had it up to here with all things Bosnian. Stuffed to the gills by a quarrel in a faraway country between people of whom you now know so much that you cannot begin to make any sense of it, you are finally losing patience. You just want the whole pack of them to stop being so bloody Balkan. If only they would learn to shape up and behave like Britons, you mutter, it would all be over by Christmas.

Fine. That's enough about the former Yugoslavia. Let's move on.

Normally, at this time of year, the autumn leaves drift by my window, the autumn leaves of red and gold. And pretty energetically they drift, too, since I live at the bottom of a blustery hill, and by the time the leaves which have fallen off at the top of the hill have reached my window, they are going at a fair old lick. They then pile themselves into big wet hummocks, which has always been the signal for the London Borough of Barnet to dispatch sturdy men with handcarts to shovel them up. Until this year: this year has brought a change of policy – do not ask why, changing policies is what councils do, it is where the fun is. This year, the bottom of the road came home last Friday to find that someone had been round and put all the leaves into big green bin-liners which had then been propped beneath the trees, in little groups of three or four, leaning together in an anthropomorphic manner pleasingly redolent of T.S. Eliot's Hollow Men, to await, the bottom of the road assumed, collection.

The top of the road did not know about any of this. Not immediately. Now, this new policy pleased the bottom of

75

the road no end, for ours is a horticulturally correct community, zealous in its organic composting, but whereas our cherished leaf-mould had hitherto been backbreakingly gleaned in dribs and drabs from our own premises, suddenly it had been delivered to us, ready wrapped, in huge portable quantities. Delivered *unto* us, you might be tempted to say, for what was this but geoponic manna? We were looking at the mulch of the gods.

There were two sacks beside my front gate. I took the first down to the end of the back-garden, and was returning for the second when my stride was broken by the unsuburban noise of angry voices barking in the street. I moved cautiously to my front hedge, and saw that my neighbour opposite had firm hold of one side of a bin-liner while someone else had equally firm hold of the other. I recognised the someone else. He was from the top of the road.

He was, that is, from the London Borough of Camden, which lies east of the road's bisecting border. And he had come for his leaves. He knew they were his leaves, because he had opened the bag and found horse-chestnut remains, and there are no horse-chestnuts west of the border. They had blown into Barnet, a point he was at pains to yell. My neighbour opposite, however, now yelled that that was neither here nor there, since what had once been there was now here due to having been bagged up by Barnet workmen paid out of council tax levied on the bottom of the road, ie, him. He had bought these Camden leaves fair and square.

A wife from the top of the road now appeared at a gallop, and put in an interesting twopenn'orth to the effect that she and her husband had been here since the days when the whole road was Cricklewood, before the Barnet–Camden border had been arbitrarily imposed, and so had the bloody conker tree. This, even a bottom-of-the-roader had to concede, was a nice point: it went to (as juridical jargon has it) the relative status of the two regions following the break-up of the former Cricklewood, and it was as moot as you could get.

It was at this fraught juncture that my neighbour opposite spotted my head in the hedge, and beckoned, in a patent plea for ethnic solidarity. I did what any honourable man would have done. I mimed a ringing phone and ran indoors. Why get embroiled? I am, after all, from the other side of the bottom of the road. A different region altogether. When I looked out of the window later, the bag had gone. I still do not know where, nor shall I inquire. I am sure it'll all be over by Christmas.

Not In Arcadia Ego

Was it or was it not an exemplary Easter Monday? Was I or was I not intoxicated, high up on Hertfordshire's sunlit hummocked Ridgeway, by the palpably thrumming regeneration all about me, things spiritual and natural mystically intertwined as they were seasonally meant to be, God's Son in His heaven, and bees, birds and buds new-risen wherever I looked? With, at my feet, a thousand different flowers.

All for sale. Which was why I was there, traipsing the

gravelled aisles of an enormous garden centre, keenly peering this way and that, my mudstained garden plan clutched in a blistered hand still smarting from the energetic preparation of the beds waiting back in Cricklewood, dug, turned, mulched, watered, and crying out, now, to befilled with stuff. What kind of stuff? All kinds. Nice tall coloured stuff at the back, nice middle-sized scented stuff in the centre, nice titchy edging stuff at the front, you know the type of thing, you've all done jigsaws.

But have you all done herbaceous borders? I had, until last weekend, not, and they turned out to be trickier than jigsaws; you haven't got a lid to guide you. True, I did have the mudstained plan, but mine is not a household name where horticulturalists forgather, and the mudstained plan just had these rough oblongs of pencilled bed on it, blotched out in coloured inks to indicate the different hues of all the stuff I thought I was after, most of which, unfortunately, had now mudstained together to give the impression that what I wished to create was a paradise of herbaceous khaki. Never mind, I had it more or less in my head. The problem was that I didn't have it more or less at my feet. I didn't have it at all at my feet, because when I said, a moment ago, that there were a thousand different flowers down there, what I should have said was that there were a thousand different things that would be flowers once they had come out. At the moment, what I had at my feet looked like a thousand little lettuces.

And then Roger appeared. I knew he was Roger, because there was a tag on his green dungarees. Roger wanted to know if he could help me. I replied joyfully that nobody could help me more, and I put him in the picture, insofar as pointing at an arrangement of shapeless khaki blobs may be said to constitute that, and Roger said: 'Why not begin with a background of *Hilarius mucus*?'

Or something like that. Whatever it was, I knew at once that we were in serious trouble, because when I asked him what *Hilarius mucus* looked like, he asked me if I was familiar with, as I recall, either *Copius gingivitis* or *Canelloni hysteria*. I told him I wasn't, and he looked a bit shaken, but tried to describe it, so I asked if it came in yellow, and it didn't, but *Polyfilla hernia* did, he said, and would go very well with what he suggested I planted in front of it, which might have been *Dubius harmonium*, or then again might not. Either way, the ideal plant to complement it as a dwarf edger would be *Insidius virus*.

Now, I shouldn't have cared as much about any of this, felt half as dumb, grinned nearly as sheepishly, had I not been rather good at Latin. If, for example, Roger had wanted to know whether Caesar was about to march his forces expeditiously to new winter quarters on this side of the river and on that, I should have rattled off the answer instantly, and even, perhaps, gone on to sing of arms and the man who first from the shores of Troy came destined to an Italian exile; but he didn't. The Latin I had been rather good at was no good at all, here. I had been taught the wrong Latin. They should have made me study Caesar's *Gallic Rockery* and Virgil's *Herbaceid*.

I went home not long afterwards, with a lot of little lettuces in the boot of the car to stick in where Roger advised they should be stuck, God knows what'll come up, but that is not the point of this piece. I have written this piece because what we do know is coming up is an election, and since education is a core subject of it, I want to make a plea for Latin to be a core subject of that. Show me a candidate who stands for Latin, and I shall show him a vote. A dead language? Not if you want live plants, it isn't.

Sitting Pretty

I have just been squatting on the Cliveden bidet. Not, sadly, the bidet *of* Cliveden, for I should have been tickled no end – as it were – to have settled my buttocks where the great and good once settled theirs; to have savoured just the merest snatch of how it must have felt, in 1963, to be Christine Keeler, staring at the golden taps and wondering what a nice girl like her was doing in a joint like this. Waiting, perhaps, for the War Minister, John Profumo, to bang on the door and inquire whether she was going to be all bloody day in there. But this bidet of mine wasn't in Cliveden, it was in Islington. It was only called the Cliveden. It wasn't even connected, let alone well. And I had my trousers on.

I had them on when I sat on the Sandringham, too. Do not begin to think about what I began to think about when I sat on the Sandringham. Though, mind you, it wasn't half as unnerving as what I thought about when I sat on the Cottage. That is another bathroom suite in the Armitage Shanks range. So is the Tiffany. And the Lichfield. And the Claudette. There they all were in the Islington showroom, in serried rank, set up and twinkled to their best by loving hands eager for them to appeal to the potential owners who strolled, and stared, and touched, and murmured, and pondered. It was a little like Battersea Dogs Home, except for the imploring eyes. That and the fact that if you are looking for a new dog, you do not try sitting on it.

The assistant was not entirely happy about the sitting. In truth, I was not that happy myself, because I was wearing my brown trilby: readers who may occasionally have spotted my front-page mugshot in this hat will perhaps appreciate my unease better than those who haven't, but even these latter may be able to empathise. One does not cut much of a dash sitting on a bidet in a brown trilby. And, since you suggest, one cuts even less of a dash by taking it off and sitting on a bidet with a brown trilby on one's knee. I cannot explain why this is so. You had to be there.

I did, anyway. I had to be there because we are having a new bathroom built, and there is no point ordering new bathroom furniture without trying it out, checking its comfort, all that, so while my wife lay in a number of baths, I sat on the other stuff. That is why the assistant was not entirely happy, because what his elegant showroom had been set up to show was his goods at their very best, looking just as they did in the smart glossy brochure, and in that brochure Armitage Shanks, though it had chosen to include a slim girl in a small towel coming out of the shower, had not chosen to include a plump man in a big hat sitting on the bidet. You could tell how unentirely happy the assistant was by looking at him while he was looking at the other potential customers looking at me, and, as the result, probably becoming less potential by the second.

To say nothing of the fact that, whenever I sat on something new, we had to talk about it. We had to talk about what, both male and female, had to get washed, and whether what I was sitting on was up to these tasks irrespective of gender – the Claudette for example, and despite its name, has, for a man, a very useful indentation of the rim which is absent from, surprisingly, the Cottage; but then again, the Cottage incorporates a soap recess, which the Claudette ignores – and the assistant, though excellent in every other way, was not quite up to discussing with a man sitting below him in a brown trilby how best, for example, to get his works over the rim of the Cottage in order to take advantage of the soap dish absent from the works-friendly Claudette.

Though none of this – it was, after all, man-to-man – was quite as tricky for him to handle as the questions I was required to ask on Mrs Coren's behalf, regarding spray-spread, jet power and so on, not least because Mrs Coren's head kept suddenly reappearing around us as she sat up in different baths, and the assistant was clearly unsettled by the risk of her overhearing something which concerned her intimately.

It didn't bother me, that. It served her right for insisting on testing only the baths because, she said, it would be embarrassing for her to do the bidets. I fail to see why. She doesn't even own a hat.

Tuning Up

They came to take the piano on Friday. They brought it down the stairs from the landing where it had stood for 25 years, and it went bong as it hit every step, but not a bong any musician could have put his finger on, because it had been out of tune for 20 of those years, and if you put your finger on it, the notes that came out belonged to it alone.

After they had got it down the stairs, they heaved it on to a little cart to wheel it up the garden path to their van, and

I walked behind, though lacking an old cock linnet, to see it off. It was a bit like a cortège. One or two neighbours watched – neighbours always watch a removal van – but they didn't say anything, because there is something about a piano leaving a house that begs discretion. Has the owner gone broke, has he gone deaf, are we watching divorce proceeds being distributed to the musical one?

It was none of these, it was simply that the piano was clapped-out. It had in truth never been very clapped-in; we had bought it for fifty quid in 1972 for the children to learn, but they learnt very little, except that you don't get much of a piano for fifty quid. It then stayed in the upstairs hall so that I could use it to tune my banjo, though as the piano was out of tune, the banjo was warped, and my ear is tin, I was never able to play anything that anybody could recognise, except parts of the slow movement of *Polly Wolly Doodle*. Musicologists among you may be surprised to learn that *Polly Wolly Doodle* has a slow movement, but that is only because you have not seen my fingering technique. I have to stop after each chord to have a cigarette and work out where to put my fingers for the next one. So, a few days back, I asked a man round to tune the piano, and he said it wasn't worth tuning, let it go.

I came indoors again after they had driven away with my quarter of a century, feeling a bit glum because it seemed as though the piano had been delivered only about five minutes earlier, and I went up to look at the spot where the piano had stood, and there was this amazingly thick oblong of untrodden carpet with a lot of stuff on it which had, over the years, fallen off and behind the piano, snapshots, bits of Lego, marbles, Christmas cards, wizened toffees, an Action Man's head, three light-bulbs, an arrow, what might once have been the newt that climbed out of Victoria's aquarium in, I think, 1980 – and a book.

The book was the fitness manual of the Royal Canadian Air Force. I had never seen it before. I do not know anyone in the RCAF, I hardly even know anyone who is fit, and I could come to no other conclusion than that Giles, at about 10, had decided either to escape piano lessons by running away to Toronto and becoming a fighter pilot, or to get himself fit enough to knock his piano teacher about. And then I opened the book. It was a revelation. It was the fitness book I had been looking for all my life. It said you did not have to go to gyms, jog for miles, buy exercise bikes or rowing machines or weights, you could get fit by answering the telephone or putting your hat on.

Thanks to isometrics. Isometrics was a muscle-stress technique whereby every physical action you took was done with total effort: you lifted a phone as if it weighed a ton, you put your hat on as if Arnold Schwarzenegger were trying to lift it off, with the result that you not only drove blood oxygenated to Bollinger effervescence throughout your body, you also transformed that body into a rippling powerhouse able to see off Canada's enemies without even getting into your plane.

Drawbacks? Social only. I was on the phone when my wife got home, and she was haggard with concern by the time I rang off (what's happened, your knuckles were white, your veins were standing out, you're covered in sweat) and when friends came for bridge on Sunday and I went out between rubbers to get drinks, I could hear their fraught mutters (is he all right, he closed that door as if 2 Para were trying to push it open, he's gripping his cards like a madman, his face went purple during that last contract), but you ignore such things if you're turning yourself into a titan. Any day now, I shall buy another piano, just so the neighbours can watch me carry it indoors.

Shall I Call Thee, Bird?

Tomorrow will be a very big day. Tomorrow will be just about as big as days get. Tomorrow will be the dawn of a new era. That is because tomorrow will be the era of a new dawn.

Yes, from tomorrow, each and every one of you, wherever you live, will be able to dial 0891 555178 and hear the dawn chorus. You will be able to lie snug in your cot, poke your keypad, and listen to chiff-chaff and willow-warbler, cuckoo and robin, blackbird and woodpecker, nightingale and tit, all at it like knives. You will, moreover, not be required to do this at dawn, for it is a round-the-clock service, and should you so wish you can listen to the dawn chorus prior to turning in, and thus get it out of the way in good time, or, if you have had a heavy night and slept late, you will be able to dial the dawn chorus at noon, having missed nothing.

For this unprecedented privilege, you will owe your heartfelt thanks to the Royal Society for the Protection of Birds, who set it up, and £1 to BT, who saw the RSPB coming. It is a small price to pay, especially as the RSPB also throws in a Mr Peter Holden, who tells you, as they severally trill, what each component of the dawn chorus is: I have heard a preview tape, and he points out, for example, that what has just exploded in the bush behind him is a wren, and that the great tit is the one which sounds like a bicycle pump, a thoughtful observation for listeners who might otherwise have grown concerned at the possibility that Mr Holden's Rudge had run over a broken jamjar while he was pedalling bravely through the aubadal chill, waving his tape-recorder on all our behalves, in hot pursuit of a finch.

The tape has the further great virtue of lasting less than two minutes. It thus differs markedly from the real thing in – to pluck an example at random – Cricklewood, where, thanks to street lighting visible from Hale-Bopp and passing cars blasting the ghetto all night, dawn begins at sunset, so that, down here, disorientated tits may start pumping their tyres up at any time, and wrens go bang on an entirely capricious basis, never mind flocks of magpies which can bring light sleepers suddenly jack-knifing upright from their sacks at half-past three.

From tomorrow on, however, it will be possible to stick earplugs in, insulating you from all this racket, get a good night's kip, and phone the dawn chorus while you're shaving. Nor, I very much hope, will BT's caring enterprise stop there: how very pleasant it would be, in spring, to phone the Croaking Frogline, or in autumn, particularly after hunting goes to its inevitable doom, to dial a nostalgic two minutesworth of horn, hooves, baying and dismemberment. Which is not, of course, to ignore the ethnic multiplicity of Britain: I myself have many friends and neighbours, now branched poignantly far from their exotic roots, who would, I'm certain, relish the opportunity to ring some 0891 number for the sunset chorus of okapi padding down to the water-hole, the lion's roar, the hippo's yawn, the rhino's belch, while others yearn to hear again the crash of tigers through the Bengali undergrowth or the redolent note – not unlike a bicycle pump, actually – of an elderly koala regurgitating a eucalyptus leaf.

As for myself – and I speak here as both an animal lover and a BT shareholder – I should most like to be able to phone a dog. I have always wanted to keep a dog, but they're a frightful liability, they have to be schooled, they have to be walked, they have to be vetted, they have to be groomed, they bite people, they chase cats, they foul footpaths, they eat that ghastly jelloid muck you have to spoon out for them, and this strikes me as a great deal of trouble to go to just to enjoy their companionship. But having a dog on the other end of the phone whenever you wanted would be just the ticket: if you felt lonely, you could ring it up, it would bark, it would pant, it would bring sticks to the phone, you would say good boy, good dog, all that stuff, and there'd be no hairs on the furniture or coppers ringing up to say they'd just prised it off the A41. I shall give BT a bell right now. It pays to talk.

How Much Is That Doggie In Your Pocket?

As a lone columnist, I have, like Blanche Dubois, always depended on the kindness of strangers. I perch in this Cricklewood eyrie, banging on to a world I cannot see, whose population I do not know, hoping against hope that they do not object to being banged on to, and thus pitiably grateful for the slightest indication that that hope is not, in both senses, vain. And should the indication ever be more than the slightest, a hot flush suffuses my raddled cheek, my little heart goes pit-a-pat, and upon each eyelid a bright tear trembles. So you see what you have done, Mrs Alice Maynard, with your Tamagotchi.

Or, rather, my Tamagotchi, which is what it is now that Mrs Maynard has so very generously sent it to me. She did this because, a fortnight ago, I wrote that I had always wanted a dog but none of the headaches that went with it, and suggested that BT, which had just released its dawn chorus service for bird-lovers, now set up a dogline so that people like me could have a dog to talk to. But Mrs Maynard had already gone much farther than that: she had gone, a month before, as far as Tokyo, and when she returned she brought with her a big bag of Tamagotchis for friends and relatives; and one, this extraordinarily compassionate lady decided after reading my column, for me.

It is a dog I can carry in my pocket. It is the size of a quail's egg. Indeed, it could be a quail I could carry in my pocket, if I had always wanted a quail but none of the headaches that went with it, or a cat, or a gerbil. It could be My Extremely Little Pony. For the Tamagotchi is a cybernetic pet, a tiny electronic sphere which the owner has to nurture if it is to thrive and love him back: it wails if it is virtually hungry or virtually unhappy, stopping only when the owner presses the little buttons which feed or comfort it, it grows virtually fat if it is overfed, it gets virtually messy if its pleas to evacuate its virtual bowels go unheeded, and if not kept a close, caring eye on, it can have up to eight different virtual accidents, any of which could kill it.

Oh, Mrs Maynard, dear kind Mrs Maynard, what have you done? My dog is sitting on my desk as I write; it has been fed, it has had a pee, and it now seems to be contentedly sleeping, but you can never be sure, any moment now it could suddenly wake up and run under a bus, it could jump out of the window, it could get eaten by a python, my life will never be the same. If it were a real dog, I could put it in the garden and get on with my work, but if you put a

Tamagotchi in the garden and went back into the loft, it could squeal, vomit and tread on a landmine and you would never know.

And there are more distressing ramifications yet, are there not, Mrs Maynard? I never knew much about the Japanese, I knew they had a taste for raw fish, short poems, and labour-intensive roadbuilding, and that was about it, but now you tell me that they have ten million Tamagotchis, and love them, and depend upon them for their happiness.

How long, then, before Nippon comes up with cybernetic children, so much less risk and hassle, so much more certainty of filial devotion and reward, and how long before such electronic virtuality spreads, as so many Japanese initiatives do, westwards?

Worse – though you were not to know it – your generous gift arrived on a very unsettling day indeed, when two other quantum long jumps took off from the board to land who knows where: not only did BSkyB and BT go into partnership to initiate interactive television shopping so that none of us need ever leave his domestic premises again, but the Deep Blue computer trounced Garry Kasparov, the smartest human being in the world.

So even as I send thanks to you, Mrs Maynard, I have to say that it is thanks to you that I have seen the future, and, God help us, it virtually works. Any day now, man will be able to sit in his solitary cubicle with his dogs in one pocket and his kids in the other, feeding, clothing and entertaining himself from the screen before him, and playing everything from cribbage to rugby league against the best the cybernetic world has to offer.

What shall we call this ideal? Would virtual hara-kiri do?

What Did You Do In The War, Daddy?

Here's a do. A Suffolk lady has written to tell me that I am the spitting image of my father – though I look, of course, much older. Yes, the 'of course' will, of course, bother you, just as it has already bothered me in more ways than it could ever bother you, for why should she assume it to be only natural that I should look much older than my father? Because, of course, she last saw him when he was far younger than I was when she last saw me. That is why I am bothered in more ways than you.

When did she last see my father? In 1944. A mere 53 years before she last saw me, because she last saw me a week ago, on *Call My Bluff*, a little pension plan of mine with which BBC I is cluttered each weekday at noon. She had not seen it before; normally, she confides, she watches Richard and Judy, whoever they are, but last Tuesday she inadvertently switched channels, and found herself watching my father, looking much older and (though she did not say it) being a silly arse. It did not take her long, mind, to twig that it was not my father, because had it been my father, he would have looked even older than that. He would have looked 85.

Had, that is, he not died when he was 76.

My correspondent does not know that my father is dead. Indeed, the main reason she wrote to me at the BBC was to find out whether he was alive, because she lost contact with him in 1944, so one of the sad things I have to do is inform her that we all lost contact with him in 1988. At least, it will be if I write back: that is my dilemma, and it is compounded by the fact that even if he is no longer with us, she would, she hints, very much like to meet me. She would like that because she and my father were, she says, very close, once.

Do you, dear reader, feel a drift moving within catchable reach? It is 1942, and my father has just been stationed at RAF Stradishall, where Bomber Command has put him because Arthur Harris has decided that if he left my father at home with his wife and four-year-old son, things might swing Adolf's way. My father is 30. My correspondent (now 77) is 21. There is a war on. My father might not come back from it.

The question, posed for me in 1997 by this letter, is where, exactly, might he not have come back from? Germany or Suffolk? Though he did finally come back from both, it is nevertheless all rather unsettling, for just how close is very close? Were there, in short, times during those two years together when there was no daylight at all between my father and my correspondent? You will cry, oh grow up, your parents are now both dead after a life of devoted inseparability interrupted only briefly, half a century ago, how much can it matter if a little blissful advantage was taken of that interruption? You are mistaken in crying this, however, because that is not what bothers me. What bothers me is the thought that if I do write back, break the news that my old man is no longer with us, and am therefore invited irrefusably to meet her in his place, not only will it be very peculiar for both of us, it is bound to be singularly unsettling for her.

For I am doomed to tread on her dreams. I am the bald middle-aged civilian whom the dashing young airman would have deteriorated into had he opted for Suffolk. If I write back, I shall have to sit opposite her, nattering nervously, while she toys with her scone and wonders sadly why she has kept that fading snapshot in some covert

91

drawer, gazing at it now and then, down the long arches of the years. She will glance up at me, smiling wanly, as dreams of what might have been dissipate forever in the presence of what ineluctably is.

Either that, or she will suddenly lash out with the serious handbag old ladies invariably carry and leave me measuring my length on the floorboards of Ye Olde Copper Kettle among the shards of shattered crockery. Because anyone can tell from her letter that my old man never once tried to get in touch with her after 1944, so there is more than an outside chance that she's been waiting 53 years to get her own back.

Knock On Any Door

I hope you'll agree that, during the ten years of my perching here, I have never abused the hospitality of this column; except, of course, in the liberty I take of bending ears which might be far more profitably turned to this great organ's deeper voices. I have never, that is, begged my readers help to sort out this or that, as other hacks often do, albeit in return for a magnum of Krug or a couple of tickets to Alton Park. Unable to put my finger on an elusive quotation, say, or find a good trattoria in Warrington, or tune my French radio to *Test Match Special*, or stop my dog eating phone-books, I have always chosen to do my own research, rather than send caring readers rushing pell-mell to the letterbox.

But today I'm compelled to break the resolution of a decade. I need to find out not only who Mr F.D. Morton is, but also why I have his office door, and, equally important, why that door says he's a bastard; and there is nowhere to turn for information like that except to a reader who might just have it. And if that reader happens to be Mr F.D. Morton himself, I can only crave his forgiveness for my telling the world what his door thinks of him, but urge him to write in anyway, to save my sanity. It has just occurred to me, mind, that if his door has got it right, Mr F.D. Morton may be too much of a bastard to get in touch with me by letter but enough of a bastard to get in touch with me by fist, but that is the kind of risk all seekers after truth are doomed to run.

Another kind which one of them is doomed to run is the risk of boring witless the readers whose hospitality he has already abused, by banging on about his skip. Nobody wants to hear about his skip, they have all had skips of their own, they know about skips, they have all been awoken by things that go bump in the night and have run to the window to observe that the thing was yet another moonlit lavatory bowl which had either just appeared in their skip or just disappeared from it, and they have all then gone back to bed to lie sleeplessly wondering who, exactly, were these people who loped the night with lavatory bowls. Or radiators. Or mattresses. The people who have turned the urban skip into a sort of inert Robin Hood, an entrepôt redistributing lavatories and radiators and mattresses from those with too many of them to those with too few.

And now mine has received a door, sometime between last midnight and breakfast, a panelled one, in cream, no knob or hinges, but garnished with three messages, two mounted professionally on little gilt plaques which say 'Mr F.D. Morton' and 'Knock and Enter' and a third, sprayed on erratically in black, which says 'Bastard!'

I have been thinking about this all day, and got nowhere. At one end of that nowhere stands the shadowy figure of Mr F.D. Morton: what is he, that he is knocked and entered upon? A schoolmaster? A civil servant? A surgeon, even? In the middle of the nowhere stands the shadowy figure of the sprayer: what made him reach for the aerosol? Had he just been expelled, for imponderable transgressions? Had he just been kicked out of the DSS office for claiming benefit for nine aliases? Had he just left hospital with the wrong leg cut off? Is it within one of these scenarios that Mr F.D. Morton's alleged bastardy lurks? Then again, there is the far end of nowhere, where stands the shadowy figure of the person who threw the door in the skip: why did he do it? He cannot be the victim of Mr F.D. Morton, because a victim would not spray 'Bastard!' on a door and then tear it off and skip it, he would want to leave it there as long as possible. It cannot be the building's owners, they would merely repaint the door. And though the only other candidate would seem to be Mr F.D. Morton himself, I cannot believe, however mortified he might have been to discover his door's desecration, that he took it off and carried it through the night to my skip. A man with a gilded plaque who has to be knocked before being entered upon is surely not the sort to risk being apprehended by the Old Bill at three in the morning, carrying a stolen door with his name on it.

So I am, forgive me, forced to invite answers, on a post-card. The first correct entry will receive a door. Provided it doesn't disappear tonight.

Poets' Corner

You find me, this morning, fraught with imponderability as to why Barratt, described in their brochure as Britain's Premier House Builder, should have sent me that brochure in the first place. Was it because they thought I might be looking for a second place? A bucolic weekend bolthole, say, far from the bustling peripolitan chic of Cricklewood? Or even somewhere to replace Cricklewood altogether, given that, for all its legendary boons, it is noticeably short of the lakes, golf courses, and lush greensward of Collingtree Park, identified (by Barratt) as the finest and most prestigious location in the entire Northampton area?

Or is it simply that Barratt believe that, however content I am in my current premises, with no thought of upping sticks, this thought might nevertheless be put into my head by the news that at Collingtree Park they have created a literary environment whose atmosphere a hack would find irresistible, rich as it must be in regenerative stimulus for an imagination worn to a frazzle by 40 years at the rock face? For the Collingtree Park Estate – described as A Premier Collection – is composed of houses called Wordsworth, and Tennyson, and Longfellow, and Coleridge. These, it should be noted, are not individual dwellings, but individual styles: some have been built, but others will be added as the development grows, which means that if you move quickly you may, for £379,850, snap up Early Wordsworth, a period any A-level student will tell you found him in prime nick, but if instead you dither until you end up with Late Wordsworth, when the old twerp had bumbled into rickety disorder, you might well find yourself regretting that you didn't go for the bargain Longfellow at £261,500.

Which – though it lacks the keynote pond fronting the Wordsworth, inviting purchasers to row back and forth across their miniature Grasmere, trailing clouds of glory, until it is time for the pondside daffs to sprout up for a bit of a dance – has enough bespoke features of its own to fill the head with Henry's rollicking rhythms as one potters his premises: *See the fully fitted kitchen. Each appliance integrated, Note the seamless double-glazing, Finest and the most prestigious, Let us look now at the garden, Lo! its broad and sunny aspect, Lo! its wealth of shrubs and borders . . .*

It has only a double garage, mind. The Wordsworth has a treble. I don't know why this should be, he got along at Dove Cottage, as I recall from my school visit, with a ramshackle outhouse. God knows what Barratt were thinking about, one each for William and Dorothy, possibly, with a spare in case Southey drove over, although he could always stay across the road at the Coleridge (£279,950), which also has two, unless, of course, a person from Porlock has turned up unexpectedly.

Why the Coleridge, incidentally, should be £10,000 more than the Tennyson, I cannot guess, except that, from the brochure, the Tennyson looks, stylistically, to be something of a dog's breakfast; surprising to find that so meticulous a prosodist should have not only an asymmetric double-front, one side flat and bricky, the other stuccoed with a bay, but also two titchy fake-Tudor windows over a garage topped by a roof unappealingly lower than the rest of the place. Hardly what one would expect of a man who could nail together an item as tricky as *Ulysses* with not a syllable out of kilter.

Stop this. We know that Barratt aren't thinking about poetry at all, but seeking merely to confer upon their properties the property of traditional quality associated with names hallowed by blackboard consensus. Barratt, like all the other big developers, have ever truffled the heritage for their themed estates, unearthed Drakes and Wellingtons and Marlboroughs, Constables and Gainsboroughs and Turners, all to endow their instant mock-villages with spurious tone. Pressing the culture's immortal poets into service is entirely consistent; indeed, given the plummeting state of that culture, it is quite possible that, any day now, it will be the sole remaining means of ensuring their immortality.

This is the way the world ends, not with a bang but a Wimpey.

Sound And Fury

Though it has figured in no major commemorations, indeed, as far as I'm aware, in no commemorations at all, it is now exactly 50 years since my late grandfather took me into his Manor House garden and firmly pointed my ear north by north-east. Please note the capital letters on Manor House: I should not want you to be misled into picturing my late grandfather as some major seigneurial figure, required by hallowed tradition to schlep the future Viscount Coren into the rich rolling greensward of his ancient seat to do that ritual thing to the lad's ear which had been done at the age of nine to all his great family's heirs since the time of Coren the Wake.

Manor House was, and remains, a blot of semi-detached north London premises huddled around the eponymous Tube station which is the grubby hamlet's only building of note.

Given this, why on earth should we be commemorating the thing with the ear? We should be commemorating it not because of what the ear was made to do, but because of why it was made to do it. The ear had been pointed north by north-east so that it could hear Heligoland go bang, 300 miles away. For Heligoland, younger readers should know, was not always a mere sea-area, noteworthy only when winds reached Force 9, backing southerly later; it was, until the summer of 1947, a German fortress. An instant later, it wasn't; for Britain had blown it up in what remains to this day the biggest non-atomic explosion there has ever been. A rare national achievement, well worth a Golden Jubilee, in my view, especially as it happened in my hearing. That was why my grandfather took me into the garden and pointed my ear towards it. Half a century on I still hear the far rumble. It set dogs off. It rattled casements. People cried: 'Blimey!'

Indubitably, had he then existed, Alf Garnett would have joined them, if only via what we in the column trade call a link. For we come now to Warren Mitchell, who is so hopping mad at the din penetrating his garden from the open-air concerts a mile away at Kenwood House that he has complained to English Heritage, which runs them. Mr Mitchell says that he was subjected to 'a weekend of hell' which prevented al fresco conversation. I do not know what was being played – the last time I went to Kenwood it was Mozart divertimenti, actually composed as a background for social chatter; though not, of course, Mr Mitchell's, which may well be more worth listening to than a lot of old crotchets – but I do know that he has pointed his finger at the true disturber of his peace, which is not the hell of music, but the hell of wattage.

New wattage, that is. Old wattage was fine. For a full century after it was discovered lying about and put to use, it behaved impeccably. Even when, later, it was poked into gramophones and radios, and thus given the chance to annoy people, it never did. This wasn't, as the more technical among you will understand, because the watt was decent, but because it was big. You could get only a handful into what are now called sound-systems, whose volume was thus contained within an acceptable territory. But a few years back, the Japanese, I think it was, invented the extremely tiny watt, and were thus able to fill a sound-system the size of a shoe-box with enough watts – if, say, driven through a neighbourhood at 3am in a purple Cosworth Ford – to shatter windows from 200 metres. And given the millions of watts that could now be shoved into a really big box nailed to the Wembley stage, a bass guitar was able to produce so much reverberation that, five miles away in Cricklewood, chimneys toppled.

Fine, I have no problem with technological advance, I accept that any day now Alfred Brendel will be able to tinkle so amplified an ivory that the Waldstein will become the first sonata to buckle the plates on Mir; my only problem is with the audience. Why do today's listeners demand music to be detonated at a level likely not only to leave their eardrums hanging in threads but peace to be laid waste for miles around? All else apart, were Heligoland to be blown up today – during, say, an Oasis gig in Knebworth – nobody in Manor House would ever know.

Water Hazard

Someone very dear to me has just been killed by a golf ball. I am still in shock. I was the one who discovered the corpse. I discovered it soon after I discovered the golf ball, because it was the golf ball which first came to my notice, being more noticeable than the corpse beside which it was floating. Since a shrewd guess will now be forming in your imagination, I suppose I should confess that, when I say very dear to me, I exaggerate somewhat: you cannot call two quid dear, even though it would probably be a fiver by now: the body is a lot bigger than it was six years ago when I carried it home with nine others in a plastic bag from Hendon Fishworld, in addition to which goldfish prices have doubtless shot up along with everything else. But anyway, dear or not, we have shared the same garden since 1991, it in the pond, I on the rim, and have grown as close to one another as those circumstances and our differing species permit; and while I may agree that had it been the fish who discovered me in the pond, dead of a golf ball, it might not have gone into shock, I cannot accept that the loss of a close fish is in any way mitigated by the possibility that the affection was unrequited. Especially when the loss is exacerbated by its nature.

Someone killed the fish. Not in self-defence – I rather doubt that the fish leapt from the pond and set about a passing golfer, forcing him to protect himself with the first weapon that came to hand – but either deliberately or unwittingly, and I want the culprit nailed. For myself (and it has to be myself, I am not walking into my local nick with a dented goldfish and a Dunlop 65 and demanding to see the Chief Superintendent of the Serious Fish Squad), I am

100

pretty certain that it cannot be the former: were some kind of crackpot stalking Cricklewood's sporadic wetlands and hurling golf balls at their fauna, I think I should have heard. I believe it to be another kind of crackpot; a conviction sustained, furthermore, by two other telling pieces of evidence, one in the guttering of my garden shed and one at the foot of my acacia: along with the carpicidal Exhibit A, they would seem to constitute incontrovertible proof that, out there beyond my back wall, some madman is playing golf.

The question is, if I am going to stand any chance of nailing him, how far beyond? Did he, that is, tee off with a driver to reach my premises from a couple of hundred yards away, or take only, say, a Number 8 iron from half that distance? Or might it have been no more than a sand-wedge, chipping into my pond from another garden a mere street away? Did he stand there, bunkered perhaps in a neighbour's sandpit or stymied behind a plastic elf, and did he finally swing, ready to cheer his deft escape, only to see the arcing ball plummet into the notorious hazard known throughout golfdom as Coren's Pond? And what about Coren's Gutter and Coren's Tree? Was that him on two earlier rounds? Or does he play with a couple of equally inept madmen? Might they, indeed, be a foursome, one of them either too incompetent to clear my wall, or competent enough to clear my house? Where, if the latter, did this one go after that? Is the green somewhere across the road, beyond my frontage? I know only that my garden isn't the green, I have looked for a hole in my lawn, but though there are, of course, several, there is none that seems large enough. Certainly none with a flag in it.

You see, do you not, where deduction ends yet nailing fails to start? Since I do not know where in the notional fairway my garden lies, I have no idea where this swine, these swines, is/are shooting from. I do not know when they do it, I have heard no one, I have seen no one, and may never do either, especially as their balls have been left where they lay, suggesting, perhaps, that my garden was never the target at all, merely the victim of three wild slices at the dog-leg fourth up the road.

Then again, I suppose it's always on the cards that he/they heard the unmistakable noise of gutta-percha meeting goldfish, twigged that a major crime had been committed, and slunk away like the poltroons they are. I hope so. I hope they have been put off their stroke for good. There are nine more dear ones in the pond, and they have had enough of golf.

White Elephant

A s a leading medieval scholar, I had of course long been familiar with that plangent metaphor from Dante's best-known work, *The Oxford Dictionary of Quotations*: 'In the middle of the road of our life, I came to myself within a dark wood, where the straight way was lost.' I had not only long been familiar with it, I had as long trusted that it would be my crutch and succour when I myself struck the age at which much more than one's abdomen goes pear-shaped: I would, that is, feel far less solitary in my own midlife crisis with the knowledge that, seven centuries earlier, Dante had been there before me.

It has not worked. Though I have suddenly come to myself to find the straight way so lost that I no longer know how to eat, how to drink, how to walk, how to sleep, how to relate to my family, how to keep old friends or make new ones, or even what to do if a man comes to read the meter or an insect scuttles in behind him, it has not worked. It has not worked because, for all his genius, Dante didn't have the first idea about fitted Axminster. Especially in cream.

A quarter of a century ago, when I was so far from the middle that I didn't even know there was a wood, we moved into this house. Its floors and staircases were clad throughout in dark-brown carpet, which suited us very well, since we had toddlers who spilled things, threw things, brought things up, and dragged in from street and garden things the dog had so far neglected to. They didn't drag in things the cat had neglected to, because the cat dragged in only things that ran about, briefly, until the cat was ready to put a stop to it. The toddlers didn't do this because they had things of their own which ran about after their cages had been opened, and until the cat was ready to put a stop to that, too. But we never minded, because the brown carpet was a dab hand at unnoticeably soaking up pee, blood, vomit and the rest, with a bit of help from other dabbing hands enabling us to preen ourselves on being the sort of unfussy parents whose offspring would not one day end up supine on shrinks' couches, with their trembling legs straight up in the air so their shoes didn't dirty the fabric.

We were also great hosts: guests could stomp in with muddy galoshes and dripping brollies and start drinking right away, so that there was bags of spilling time until they had to stagger to the table and begin knocking plates to a carpet canny enough to allow the soup to extinguish the cigarette butts, before imperceptibly absorbing it. It also took nosebleeds in its stride.

And then, last week, it went. Twenty-five years of domestic archaeology were lifted and envanned; and what was devanned was its cream replacement. For, having arrived at the middle, we decided to refurbish the wood, and we felt that cream would be just the ticket. It is. It is the ticket to the rest of the wood, where the straight way is lost. I have lived with it for a week, and I do not know where to turn.

I dare not smoke, except in the kitchen, and if the doorbell goes I have to stub out and tiptoe sockily across the cream hall in case the kitchen floor has left a tomato pip on my shoe; and when I open the door, I dare not let anyone in who does not remove his shoes. Worse yet, since my children have keys and could walk in at any time before I could stop them, I dare not go upstairs.

I used to eat upstairs, in my study, my bed, my bath; a pizza, a cocoa, a brandy. I dare not do that now, or carry our breakfast tray there, wobbling up cream stairs, across cream landings, into cream rooms. I dare not carry anything, since I dare not put it down, lest there be something transferably uncream on its underside. If it rains I dare not step out, not just because I dare not step in again, but because a burglar might break in before wiping his feet. Yesterday a spider got away with murder, or rather, without it.

My dreams of grandtoddlers have become nightmares, I can never have another pet, I have thrown my last party and eaten my last mango. I live in terror of everything, except dandruff; terror no one else can begin to imagine, for – as even the uncarpeted Dante knew – 'com'è duro calle lo scendere e'l salir per l'altrui scale'. How hard is the way up and down another man's stairs.

104

What's Eating Me?

Throughout my life – much of which has been spent staring vacantly out of windows, propitious circumstances for woolgathering – I have toyed with various daft fantasies as to how I should like that life to have left its mark after it had no throughout left. As a small boy, I favoured something military: Coren's Last Stand, perhaps, Coren's Drift, the Charge of the Coren Brigade, even the War of Coren's Ear. A little later, a sporting memorial seemed sweeter: the Coren Riband, the Coren End at Lord's, the Coren Flop. Since, however, such honours could come only as testament to a prowess to which I soon found it was pointless to aspire, I moved, at 13, having had a poem about acne accepted for the school magazine, to daydreams of the Corenic Simile and the Coren Memorial Theatre; until I went up to what I hoped might someday be called Coren College, whereupon I threw in, for good measure, the Coren Chair, Coren's Uncertainty Principle, and, admittedly a long shot, Duke Coren's Library.

Things went a mite quiet after that, as professional and domestic life were forced to preoccupy themselves with busy reality; though there was, of course, the odd inert spell when the wool gathered into baggy shapes like *Coren's Weekly Advertiser*, the Coren Method (a system of bringing up children by shouting at them) and – until it died of what briefly made it different from its peers – the Coren Rose. But it was finally borne in upon me, and high time too, that the options for immemorial achievements had dwindled to the point where the only chance of posthumous imperishability lay in contracting, say, Coren's Syndrome or Coren's Palsy, ie, something so unfathomable that the top medical bananas would have no other course but to shake their heads, pocket their stethoscopes, and ask me if my affairs were in order.

Until, that is, last Friday, when, at the eleventh hour, a window on immortality opened; or, rather, a letterbox. A well-known cook, whom I shall not identify for reasons which will become obvious, had written to explain that she was compiling a book of new seafood recipes, and since one of these had been inspired by a piece I had written a year or so back on the difficulties of eating squid, she was very keen to name it after me. She wants to call it Gumbo Coren. I cannot, of course, preempt her by revealing the components, but I think I break no confidences when I tell you that the dish contains a lot of legs and ink.

Um. I put the letter aside, and stared out of the window. There were, no question, many noble precedents: Tournedos Rossini, Peach Melba, Sole Walewska, Omelette Arnold Bennett, all of which had unarguably conferred not only immortality but one into which umpteen subsequent generations had happily tucked, blessing the name even as they mopped up the sauce and picked their teeth for the last savoury shard.

Why, then, did I hesitate? Two reasons, differently reasonable: the first, and why I haven't named my generous would-be benefactress, is that I have no idea if her recipe, though many have been superb, is any good. I shouldn't want diners to take one mouthful, and, through it, mumble: 'My God, what is this muck?', only to be told what it was. Worse yet, given the volatile properties of some of the constituent bivalves, I shouldn't want anyone to lurch groaning to the bathroom in the middle of the night, cursing my name, nor, worst of all, my descendants to wake some far morning to banner headlines shrieking 'Lord Mayor's Banquet Devastated by Gumbo Coren, Hundreds

Rushed to Intensive Care'. But if I really come clean on this, it is the less reasonable reason which makes me the more apprehensive. Hardly a reason at all, in truth; more a sort of unease. It is the name. For we are talking perpetuity here, and I doubt I am alone in feeling that, while Brigade and Simile and College, even Peach, are beyond reproach as immortal companions, one would not wish one's patronymic to spend eternity dragging Gumbo behind it, I have therefore written to its inventor, suggesting that her dish by any other name would smell as sweet, and that, should she still wish to do me honour, I'd be more than happy with Gumbo Cricklewood.

The Cricklewood Dome

I have had a millennial vision. I hope it will be of some use. In the middle of yesternight, I suddenly found myself no longer in my bed but sitting on a starlit cloud high above this queendom's great capital; and, gazing down, I saw a vast dome shimmering like a silver Smartie beside as shimmeringly silver a ribbon of river, and all along that river and all along the thready web of roads spread out around it, I saw a million human dots trudging very slowly towards the dome, from all directions and from as far away as my elevated eyes could see.

More yet, each dot was accompanied by another, some larger than itself, some smaller, which it was pulling, or pushing, or carrying. And, as I craned to peer more closely, I saw that all this shimmering was generated not only by a hundred banks of powerful lights, serving as many television cameras, but also by the effect upon these lights of a hundred plumes of smoke, wafting hither and yon across the halogen beams, from a hundred different, and – I could just sniff – fragrant fires.

Blimey, I thought, I know what's brought this on. For I had spent the previous day both bedridden with a febrile condition much conducive to antiobiotic visions and, as the result, listlessly channel-hopping all the television that there was; and had thus seen little bits of perhaps 38 different antiques programmes, 47 different animal programmes, 83 different cookery programmes, and getting on for 121 celebrity game shows. For that is all there is on television, these days; which means, more or less, that that is what the culture is.

Having diagnosed which, I let my cloud sink lower, in hope my vision might reveal what all these folk were doing on what was, I suddenly twigged, Millennium Night. And saw that New Tony, having by this time made everything The People's Everything, had now made The People's Millennium: and the People were converging on the dome from every cranny of these islands in order to queue up for inclusion on an all-channel television programme called *The Antique Animals Cookery Game*. What they all were pushing and pulling and carrying, I could now see, were their animals: each of some 50 queues had formed behind tables postered 'Dairy Cattle' and 'Fancy Mice' and 'Talking Birds', and 'Prize Newts', and so on, at which famous experts sat, inquiring how long the owners had had this or that beast, how they had come by it, and, most important,

108

whether they had ever given any thought to how much it was worth. Not, of course, for insurance purposes, but as food. Cameras would then track dramatically in on owners staggered to discover that Dobbin, their elderly Shetland, could bring as much as 50 francs a kilo in Belgium, and that – small birds being so prized an Italian delicacy – a budgie stuffed with pine kernels might go for over two million lire in Positano, even if it had never uttered a single intelligible word.

Any sick animals were, of course, passed on to a horde of glamorous quiz-panels, where chortling celebrities were invited to guess, with wondrous hilarity and innuendo, their ailment, and have their answers judged by a major television vet, who would press a cheery bell if he thought the condition curable by Rolf Harris, and a farty buzzer if he believed the animal should immediately be put down by Anton Rodgers.

This diversion, while both uproarious and heartrending, had the further boon of allowing the necessary time for the most valuable healthy animals to be slaughtered, and then, to the finest piped music, cooked competitively by such as Gary Rhodes, Rick Stein, Delia Smith, Sophie Grigson, Keith Floyd, and as many fat ladies as could safely be mustered on the podium, with wines chosen by Oz Clarke, Jilly Goolden, Jancis Robinson, etc, dab hands all at knowing what goes best with *tabby au vin* and *gerbil suprème*, and eaten, for a major trophy, by a bevy of soap-stars under the incomprehensible stewardship of Loyd Grossman. The vision faded, but the heart stayed high. It will be not merely the most wonderful TV programme there ever was, it will be the truest defining index of our culture, and thus the dome's finest hour, as the century's supreme midnight ushers in the new millennium. Whatever that might mean.

You And Whose Army?

If I turn my head a few degrees leftwards from the screen on which I have just written the words describing what I am now doing, my eyes arrive at a shelf bearing a few framed photographs of my family at war. Not, let me quickly type, at war with one another: these are not candid snaps of domestic rows, my relatives are not at one another's throats, there is no crockery flying about.

What they are at war with is Germany. I can't, of course, see this in the photographs, my family is not shooting anyone, they are not dropping bombs, nobody is wiping a bayonet; what they are doing is taking a break from the war to smile at the camera. They are all in uniform: here is my father, no older than my son, leaning against a hut at RAF Stradishall; here is a studio group of his brothers Les (Eighth Army) and Gus (Royal Ulster Rifles), with his sisters Ann (ATS) and Sadie (Land Army); and here, next to them, is my mother's brother Sid (Middlesex Regiment), with a big bandage around the top of his head and a big grin across the bottom of it, the former a testament to his recently having been at Dunkirk, the latter a testament to his even more recently having got back from it. So, can you guess what I am wondering, half a century on? I am wondering how my Auntie Ann would have fared in a rear turret over the Ruhr, and how my Auntie Sadie would have looked with shrapnel in her forehead.

I am wondering this because George Robertson has invited me to. For the Ministry of Defence, as you, too, will have read in Monday's *Times*, is about to ask the British public whether it wants women to fight in the front line, and as a member of that public I cannot give the Defence

Secretary a straight answer until I am able to come to terms with the notion of my aunties, instead of decoking trucks or planting runner beans, parachuting into Arnhem firing their Sten guns from the hip.

And since George is unlikely ever to get a straight answer from me on this, let me instead put him a straight question: is this unprecedented soliciting of the public's tactical opinion to be taken as a pointer to the future course of Britain's military policy? Am I, that is, to assume that new Labour's zest for referendum is soon to embrace all aspects of the defence of the realm? Because if it is as short a step as it seems from choosing the sort of Armed Forces we want to choosing what we should want them to do when we've got them, then I have a considerable amount of boning-up to do.

We all have: we shall have to fill our bookshelves with *Jane's Fighting This and That*, we shall have to obtain highly detailed maps of every country in the world, and highly detailed charts of every sea, we shall have to clear out our lofts to make room for regiments of toy soldiers – of both sexes – and model tanks and guns and ships and missiles and all the deployable rest; we shall, in short, have to become tactical and strategic experts, because we are not talking here about such fripperies as single currencies or Welsh assemblies or foxhunting, we are talking about far more fraught and complex referendal decisions than those, and ones to be taken, moreover, far more snappily – as soon as, say, the newsflash breaks into *EastEnders* to inform us that the SS *Belgrano Nuevo* has just been sighted off Clacton, please ring 0345 2222 if you want to sink it, 0345 3333 if you want to wave to it, all calls charged at standard rate, or that Saddam Hussein has landed at Inverness and is marching on Prestonpans at the head of the Republican Guard, if you feel Britain should go

111

nuclear on this one, please e-mail as soon as possible to: armageddon@trident.uk.

On reflection, George, I think not. You yourself must be a brave little soldier, and defend the realm without my input. Oh, I am happy enough with the concept of The People's Party, I am more than happy with its declared vision of The People's Country, I am even ready to follow it into The People's Century, but if it is seeking my endorsement of The People's Army, it will seek in vain. Because I rather fancy that if you wish to keep the nation safe for democracy, then you have to recognise when to keep it safe from it.

The Leaving Of Cricklewood

Forgive me. I hate to be the bearer of double whammies but I have, this morning, no option: all I can pray is that you will somehow find the fortitude to bear what I bear to you. Provided, of course, that the first whammy has not already left you supine in some darkened room, gaunt and listless beneath your saline drip and waiting for a council carer to come in and massage your feet; in which event, you must not read one further word of this.

That first whammy – for those of you still standing, albeit still reeling – was borne by last weekend's *Sunday Times*, which, quite properly, gave over much of its front page to the shattering global news that Martin Amis was quitting the UK for New York, to escape media scrutiny and public preoccupation with his advances, his partner, and his teeth, to flee the new politics for which he so recently voted but with which he is now disappointed (he confesses himself nostalgic for Baroness Thatcher), to shed the 'middle-class boredom', of Britain and – since 'I have only got one big London book left to write – emigrate to where the history of the next century is already being written'.

What an extraordinary and culturally devastating coincidence! For I, too, have been suffering those self-same torments and, having come to those self-same conclusions, am determined to leave Cricklewood for good. I have only one big Cricklewood column left to write – it will address man's eternal quest to discover why, four years ago, a Barnet council workman bothered to draw a red ring around the pothole outside my house, when it remains a pothole to this day – and, as soon as it is written, I shall be off.

I have had more than enough of media scrutiny (the *Ham & High* rings up every summer to ask which paperback I am taking on holiday) and as for the public's preoccupation with my advances, every time I bring a book out someone asks me what I got for it and then nods and says he'd always wondered why I was forced to do so much daytime television, doesn't your wife work? Whereupon, my having replied that she is a doctor, he immediately rolls his trousers up and asks her to have a look at his knee, so if Martin thinks society is obsessed with his partner, let me ask him how often the radiant Isabel has been required to feel a wonky patella during her soup course while simultaneously trying to avoid the eye of the woman opposite who has clearly been stitched up, every which way, by a dodgy plastic surgeon and now, alerted by the exposed joint, wants to know whom to sue?

As for my teeth, preoccupation with these is reaching hysteria: I have this year alone had six reminders from my dentist to come in for a check-up, each more threatening than the last. Any day now I expect to hear the unmistakable noise of a man towing a drill up a garden path, so the sooner I change addresses the better.

And yes, like Martin, I am disillusioned with new Tony. It's been weeks now, and nobody in Cricklewood seems better educated, healthier, richer or more caring. All that has happened is that The Cricklewood Arms, our only middle-class pub, has changed its name to The Ferret & Firkin, which seems, so far, to have done little to lift the boredom for which it has been a byword throughout the 25 years I have been going in, having a quick pint, and going out again, without anyone looking up from the *Daily Mail* crossword.

There used, mind, to be a fairly interesting greengrocer opposite, he had once played in goal for Cyprus, but his wife left him last year and he went back to Nicosia.

So I have concluded, like Martin, that enough is enough (and here I must apologise to the Editor, who was desperate to run the story as a front-page lead until I told him that, if he did, my only column idea was this pothole with a red ring around it) and it is time to pack my traps and quit Cricklewood.

I am going where the history of the next century is already being written. I have often sat in its shimmering gridlock, day and night, rapt with envy at the radiant hypermarkets and bustling fast-food outlets and teeming wine bars of the city that never sleeps. And I, too, am nostalgic for Lady Thatcher. I shall emigrate to Finchley.

Don't Put A Gift Horse In The Mouth

Never look a gift horse in the mouth. Look it in the bowels. In the bowels is where the Greeks lurk, waiting to debouch and sack.

A free pudding arrived this morning. I did not immediately know it was a free pudding, I did not know it was any kind of pudding, I knew only that the doorbell had trilled, and that I had signed for a small yet heavy cardboard cube which I carried into the kitchen, put on the table and looked at. I now knew it had come from the United States, because it had 32 Elvis Presley stamps covering the whole of one flank; which in itself was arresting, since, set out as they were in painstaking phalanx, the effect the Elvises collectively created was of a small, silkscreened Warhol. The person who stuck these down, ran my first thought, is no ordinary person. I lifted the box again, turned it, and now saw that it carried a US Customs declaration, identifying it as 'gifted comestible bakery for personal consumption, value not more than $10'.

Knowing me as you do, you will be unsurprised to learn that I spent the next minute or so wondering just how gifted this comestible bakery might be: given the limitless ingenuity of Americans, the box could well contain, say, a dozen tap-dancing bagels, or an angel cake with a PhD in quantum mechanics or a fondant fancy which, when its glacé cherry was poked, did an impression of Groucho Marx reciting the Gettysburg Address – remote offchances, I grant you, especially for less than ten bucks, but, then again, the box bore a California postmark, so nothing was impossible.

It was time either to chuck it in a bucket of water and run, or open it. Not the easiest of choices – a gifted West Coast comestible carried by 32 obsessively arranged Elvises gives off a sharp psychopathic whiff – but I am not young, it has been a full life, my affairs are in order, and the daily was using the bucket, so I removed the wrapping paper, and prised open the lid.

Nothing went bang. Inside there was a lot of bubble-wrap, and inside that there was a lot of tinfoil, and inside that there was something not, indeed, unlike a bomb: the sort of bomb you find in animated cartoons, round, black, shiny, and with a curly thing poking out of the top; in this instance holly. It smelt of brandy. It was a Christmas pudding.

It had a card for me. The card had holly on it, too, and robins and silver bells, and a dark brown stain indicating that a long, boring flight in such tantalising proximity to booze had got the better of the card. A pity, because when I plucked the card out to discover who my distant benefactor was, all I discovered was that his/her writing had been illegibilised by the pudding's stain. Worst of all, there was no way of telling whether the card had ever carried a name or address. I say worst of all not because it meant that I could not write to thank my benefactor, it meant that, if he/she had withheld the name or address, how could I be sure that the pudding had not been sent by a distant malefactor?

There are a lot of very peculiar characters over there, mooching the Pacific shoreline and jabbering to themselves; they follow strange gods, they imbibe strange substances, they do strange things, often serially. In a culture whose legally appointed guardians once sent exploding cigars to Fidel Castro, who could with any confidence say that some unofficial crackpot, some lunatic sect, had not decided to

116

express its contempt for Christmas by filling the mails with poisoned puddings?

I know six people in California. I phoned them all, even though I had not seen them in 20 years, and asked. I have little doubt that all six subsequently hung up thanking their lucky stars that, however wacky California might be, it wasn't as wacky as England. What do I do now? I do not want to bin what might be a delicious treat from someone who loves me, but nor do I want, on Christmas Day, to walk into my dining room with a flaming item designed to snuff the lot of us out.

Have I, that is, been sent a Trojan pudding? When dotty old Ezra Pound foresaw 'new Troys that tumble, sizzling', was he perhaps thinking of Cricklewood? With crazy Americans, you can never be sure.

Little Things Mean A Lot

Iam a disappointed man. I am a disappointed man because Ken is a disappointed man, and he is a disappointed man because, while he has always been an unappointed man, there was a very good chance that, this year, he would have become an appointed one. But he has not. Ken remains as unappointed as a man can be. He still has no genitalia. It will have been no end, as it were, of a disappointment.

Ken is, of course, Barbie's significant other, and his tragedy is that for the past 36 years he has been less significant than he would like. But this year, for the first time, his hopes, at least, would have been raised: this year, and a mere week ago at that, Mattel, who manufacture the titchy couple, announced that Barbie was to be remodelled, in order to become more realistic.

She would be given not only a smaller, more credible, and, very important, more politically acceptable bust, but also a more authentic hip-waist ratio, a particular benefit of which would be, and I quote, to make it easier to get her clothes on and off. Music, one would imagine, to Ken's ears; until one rang Mattel the next day and learned that Ken's ears would remain his only boneless extremities.

How can that be, I cried, this is 1997, these are two devoted young lovers, they are role-models for millions of modern life-wise kids, yet while one of them is actually being rebuilt to facilitate kit-removal, the other is to be left with no part in all this. But the charming PR woman merely sighed, and told me that that was how maidenhead felt – an answer by which I was quite seriously thrown, until I twigged that Maidenhead was where the Mattel executives worked.

Indeed, so thrown was I by the entire experience that after ringing off I drove down to the Brent Cross toyshop to have a close look at the pair of them; whereupon it was borne in upon me that, in terms of what is required of 1997 role-models, there was more to Ken's shortcomings than didn't meet the eye. For Ken, I concluded, was as politically incorrect as it was possible, these days, to be: he was lean and muscular, he was chisel-chinned, his hair was lustrous, his skin was flawless, and the more I turned Ken this way and that, the more offended I grew, not merely in my own behalf but in my entire gender's.

How dare Mattel make only Barbie more realistic! Even if Maidenhead felt that the market was not yet prepared for an ungelded Ken, that market has the right to demand that its children be discouraged from regarding youthful hand-someness as the only criterion for desirability. Especially as it is manifestly untrue: seek the girls who look like Barbie, and where do you find them? You find them on the arms of Bernie Ecclestone and Peter Stringfellow and Bill Wyman and Paul Daniels.

Is it not time for Mattel to take account of that? If you can buy 100 accessories to make Ken more conventionally glamorous, why are not as many available to make him less conventionally so, thereby reducing the affront which the unblemished Ken represents to the nation's men? A bald patch range, say, and stick-on plastic paunches in various sizes, knees jointed so as to offer every option from bandy to knock, a large conk, with or without excrescent bristles, flat feet, and a packet of tiny transfers offering everything from liver spots and broken blood-vessels to eczemic flurries and varicose veins?

Yes, of course, there are other desiderata required to boost new Ken's desirability, and Mattel could do themselves considerable commercial good by putting these on the shelves alongside the others: a string of My Little Polo Ponies, say, a miniature suite at the Paris Ritz, two Concorde tickets to the Bahamas, a platinum credit card in Barbie's name, or, better yet, a plain brown envelope . . .

I know what you're thinking; you're thinking: why should Mattel endow Ken with all these items while continuing to keep him bereft of the one which would enable him to take advantage of them? But I'm thinking: if only Mattel can be persuaded to pursue the course of realism on which it has just so tentatively embarked, then how far off can that joyous day be when, at last, Maidenhead yields to the feeling that things should no longer be beyond our Ken?

I'd Like To Get Me On A Slow Boat To China

Today is a very big day for me. It is the last time I shall use the word Cricklewood. That is because there are 1.6 billion Chinese aboard this planet, and none of them can pronounce it. It is also the last time I shall get off a cheap crack at Chinese pronunciation.

I have taken this momentous decision because I wish to get on the right side of Gordon Brown. It is the only side to be on: there is nothing for me on the left side of Gordon Brown, since I am neither young enough to qualify for a childcare club nor old enough to qualify for a subsidised gasfire; but while that is just about all there is on Mr Brown's left side, his right side is a goldmine, and, with a bit of luck, I could soon find myself sitting on it.

Any moment now I could become a creative industrialist; because Mr Brown not only wants me to go into industry, he wants industry to go into me. He said so in his thrilling pre-Budget statement. He said he was eager for the creative arts to become a major plank of economic policy. That is why he is setting up a Creative Industries Taskforce, to chuck a billion lottery pounds at artists applying for grants from a brand new muse called Nesta. She is the National Endowment for Science, Technology and the Arts and, even as I type, I feel her presence hovering by my screen. I can smell her gravy.

In order to dip my bread in it, however, I shall have to do my part. I can no longer sit here banging stuff out for the domestic market, since that will never enrol me as a plank in our economic policy; what Gordon Brown wants is for me to become an international player, he wants me to commend myself irresistibly to overseas buyers, he wants me to bring foreign currency rolling in. He wants me to write exports.

Not easy, in my game. Were I a Parker or a Minghella, a Hirst or a Hockney, a Spice or a Gallagher, a Riverdancer or a Sleep, a Conran or a Foster, a Rattle or a Birtwistle, a Ken or an Emma, then the world would be my oyster; it would beat a path to my door, as only an oyster can, and it would be bearing big fat pearls, for me and for Gordon, too. But I do not splice film or slice sheep, I neither sing music nor dance to it, I do not design or conduct or compose or act, I do not, in short, engage in any of those industrial processes fortunate enough to transcend frontiers by speaking the common language of all humankind. I sit in a loft in the marginal parish of Cricklewood and engage in an industrial process unfortunate enough to transcend nowhere by speaking a language which daily grows less common even to those for whom it was designed.

You wouldn't believe how glum, after the Chancellor sat down, this made me. It wasn't merely the matter of disqualification from Nesta's largesse, it was also the matter of not being able to march behind Mr Brown towards the broad sunny uplands of economic triumph. How I wanted to play my part in creating the New Britain, attracting, by my industry, huge sackfuls of foreign cash to shorten waiting lists, fund schools, build homes, and make the trains run on time! But what international demand could there be for a Cricklewood wag?

And thus the melancholy days passed – until it was time for one of them to be Sunday, or, as it subsequently became, yesterday. The day, as you will instantly have calculated, before my very big day; and the day which made my very big day the way it is. For it was on Sunday that, as I listlessly turned the tonnage of newsprint, I spotted a down-page snippet which hurled me instantly from that listlessness. Did you perhaps see it, too? Did you also learn that English is now understood by one Chinese in ten? And did you work out how many Chinese that is?

It is the answer to a wag's prayer, that's how many it is. As soon as she has moved in behind her till, I shall ask Nesta for my grubstake. It will take the form of a ticket to Beijing, and the lease on a loft in one of its marginal suburbs, where I shall wait for marginal things to happen to me, jot them all down as waggishly as I am able, and, when enough have been jotted to cobble into a book, flog a copy to each and every one of China's 160 million clamouring Anglophones. Then I shall come back home again, with a penny whistle to my lip, a parrot on my shoulder, and a diddy-box full of cash for Mr Brown.

Sleeping With The Enemy

Canny as you are in the ways of this world, you will, I know, be neither surprised to hear that I receive, in an average week, some two dozen calling cards, nor envious of the giddy social whirl this information might appear to bespeak; because you receive them, too. They are not delivered on monogrammed silver salvers by periwigged flunkeys inviting us to a spot of dinner at Lady Molly's or a hand of bezique with the Earl of Edgware, they are poked through our letter-boxes, often in threes, by stubbled derelicts in shell-suits inviting us to a spot of vindaloo at the Moti Mahal or a hand of cowboy down our drains.

And while these missives vary broadly in professional quality – ranging from flimsy Roneoed offers of lanscape gardnin, through glossy triptych endorsements by smirking former ITN newsreaders of personal finance schemes which have brought early retirement aboard their own Caribbean sloops, to embossed pasteboard undertakings that every individually architect-designed kitchen carries with it a hand-written 200-year guarantee from the Filipino Secretary of State for Fitted Cupboards – all exude that same acrid pong of iffiness which alerts the more circumspect among us to reach for our bargepoles.

And, beyond any question, the iffiest of all are the invitations to alternative therapies. These do not merely pong, they quack, and while I may be unqualified to take issue with the Prince of Wales over how much good what he is graciously pleased to call complementary medicine might do to the nation's sick, I have to say that his recent enthusiastic endorsement of it has done no good at all to the nation's mats. Of late, I have noted a sudden exponential surge in invitations from countless crackpots manifestly fired by Royalist zeal who insist that they alone are in a position to triumph where conventional means have failed, and that should I ever find myself feeling a bit – if I will forgive the technical jargon – under the weather, then my only course would be to ring for an immediate appointment at the world-renowned Kilburn Karavan Klinic, conveniently parked behind Burger King, where their highly trained international staff will, following the thorough diagnosis of a rooster's entrails and a full body-scan via tuning-fork techniques discovered by the ancient Aztecs, bang aromatic nails into my flesh, wire my head up to their unique Electromagnetron, flush me through with a foaming mixture of Dead Sea water and Ariel Automatic, hang me from a peg invested with miraculous healing properties by the spirit guide of a much-loved member of the Monégasque Royal Family, and send me skipping back into the world in pristine fettle. If, on the other hand, I am too infirm to travel, the Klinic would be only too pleased to drive round to my place and do it, subject of course to petrol-money up front.

Now, though all these will, as I say, instantly be binned by the shrewd majority, there may yet lurk among my readership a desperate few suffering from ailments which have hitherto defeated conventional doctors, who may therefore be prey to such charlatans, and it is to them that today's column is principally addressed. For I have this week received not one but two invitations from soi-disant healers against whom the more gullible must especially be warned, in that both claim not only to be hypnotherapists, but also to offer a domiciliary service.

Yes, they will come round to your premises, and put you to sleep. Might we not, after the briefest reflection, conclude this to be the iffiest invitation of all? Might it not only pong and quack but also set clanging a very carillon of alarm bells? Because the unique concern here, surely, is not that hypnotism doesn't work, but that, unlike all those other catchpenny procedures, it does. Which is to say that there is undoubtedly a slim chance that you could indeed be put into a trance and awake an hour later to find your aches and pains gone. Which is also to say, to those of us canny in the ways of this world, that there is an even fatter chance that you could be put into a trance and awake an hour later to find your hypnotherapist and your silverware gone.

Money In The Hat

The man beside me was interested in Yul Brynner's hat. Indeed, he was so interested in Yul Brynner's hat that he was beside himself, too. He could hardly sit still, although he would have to try because the hat wasn't scheduled to turn up for an hour, and if the man beside me didn't sit still, with, moreover, his hands in his lap, he might easily wind up, willy-nilly, with Ingrid Bergman's earrings or Edward G. Robinson's cabin trunk. Because they do not muck about at Christie's, they are there to shift stuff as snappily as possible (in this instance last week's movie memorabilia) and every member of the huge crowd would have to take extreme care not to distinguish himself inadvertently from the rest of that crowd if he didn't want to wind up standing in the South Kensington street with Stanley Holloway's grand piano and a receipt for whatever the bidding had reached when he incautiously blew his nose.

Since you ask, I was not interested in Yul Brynner's hat. I was not even interested in Ingrid Bergman's earrings, Edward G. Robinson's cabin trunk, or Stanley Holloway's Bluthner, even though it was offered with a matching stool. I was interested only in a 10 x 8in photograph of Laurel and Hardy, signed by both, because Christmas was coming and my ideas were getting thin, and it would be just the ticket for someone dear to me, provided the ticket would be no dearer to me than the estimated £200. It was Lot 37.

At 2pm, the auctioneer said hello, and Lot 1 came up. A signed postcard of circusmonger Phineas T. Barnum. All I knew of Barnum was his observation that there was a sucker born every minute, a judgment which, when his postcard was knocked down for £403, seemed to me to have borne the test of time rather well, but the man who was interested in Yul Brynner's hat said there wasn't much Barnum about, and I said are you a dealer, and he said no, I just collect Yul, and I thought: how can a man who is interested only in Yul Brynner know how much Barnum there is about? I became so enwrapped in this that I missed Sir Henry Irving's gloves, but I recovered in time for Cole Porter's engraved cigarette case, which went for what seemed to be a snip at £300, until the man who cared only for Yul Brynner's hat told me that Cole Porter had owned 1,200 cigarette cases. Since this, surely, could not have been true of Edward G. Robinson's monogrammed cabin trunk, I confessed myself amazed when this was bought in at £170 – Edward G. Robinson, I said, *Little Caesar, Double*

Indemnity, you cannot buy a cabin trunk in John Lewis for £170, but Yul Brynner's hat-man said Edward G. Robinson was not collectable, don't ask him why. Not that I would have had time to, because suddenly it was Lot 37, and I was waving my catalogue, but I dropped out at £200, and Stan and Ollie went for £300, and I said, stone me, it's only a photo, and the man beside me said, yes, and there are probably 10,000 like that, but they're very, yes, I said, I understand, very collectable, and he said right, and I said this means there are three million poundsworth of Laurel and Hardy photographs in the world, you could swap them for HMY *Britannia*, and he said why would you want to do that?

So I shut up, and a pair of Ursula Andress's trousers went for £75, with a pair of her boots thrown in, and I said it's a funny old world, but he wasn't listening, because the next lot was the black stetson Yul Brynner wore in *The Magnificent Seven*, and the man beside me was suddenly a thing possessed, his arm going up and down like a beam engine as the bidding raced through a thousand, and two, and ... but, heartbreakingly, the thing possessed was destined never to possess the thing that possessed him, because he slumped at £4,000, the arm fell into his lap, and Yul Brynner's hat, a moment later, went for £5,175.

The man got up, and lurched exitwards. I left, too; there was no more for me there. I didn't want Richard Burton's mink coat or Sean Connery's tuxedo, I wanted only to ask the man why a Yul Brynner stetson was worth 300 Edward G. Robinson cabin trunks, but when I got outside, he was leaning on Christie's wall, dabbing at his eyes. So I hurried off, in the opposite direction. I hope he didn't stand there too long. Sleet was beginning to fall, and he didn't have a hat.

Would You Believe It?

I had been curled up here for some time, in this corner of my terminally Yuled living-room, trembling fitfully, like an ineptly nesting dormouse, among the uncleared mounds of wrapping paper, cracker shards, busted tree-balls, nutshells, needles, gnawed bones, bottles, torn crowns, stale pies, buckled squeakers and all the other post-festive detritus, and I had been racking the throbbing remnants of my brain, on the last day of 1997, in an effort to come up with something to offer my readers which might just put a spring in their step for the beginning of 1998, when the tree fell over. It fell over because my leg went suddenly to sleep – a boon which had managed to elude the rest of my body for most of the previous week – and, in straightening it to alleviate the numbness, my foot came up against the tree-light wire, and, even before the fairy had hit the floor, the idea for this column came to me.

I knew what I would offer my readers for 1998. I would offer them the chance to get out of Christmas for good. I would offer them a brief rundown, based on my wide knowledge of comparative religion, on a few other faiths to which they might sensibly convert, to avoid all this.

Judaism has considerable appeal. The soup is good, and you can keep your hat on indoors, thereby enjoying a substantial saving on fuel costs. Also, books are read back to front, which means that you do not have to plough through the whole of the new Jeffrey Archer to find out what happens. The main drawbacks to Judaism are that you will be expected to forgo lobster thermidor, tell at least three new jokes a week, and support Tottenham Hotspur.

Islam may suit you even better than Judaism, in that if

you don't want to read the new Jeffrey Archer at all, you can not only burn it, you can apply to have him shot. Furthermore, you will be in a position to take advantage of whatever you think polygamy may have to offer, although I should not advise this for anyone who has difficulty remembering anniversaries. The main drawback to Islam is that you are required to take your shoes off when entering a mosque. If it is a big mosque, it may take you all day to find them again.

Buddhism is unquestionably the religion to go for if you are bald. Nobody will ever know. You can also spend the entire day walking up and down Oxford Street without having to buy anything. Moreover, the principle of reincarnation is very attractive. You could come back with a full head of hair, or, with even better luck, as the Sultan of Brunei or Bill Gates. But then again, you could come back as Jeffrey Archer.

Hinduism, likewise, has both major pros and cons. You do not have to find your own wife, which will save you a small fortune in flowers, perfume, chocolates and jewellery, but you have to stay open until midnight, all week, because you can never tell when a non-Hindu might want to come in and buy flowers, perfume, chocolates and jewellery. You may also have to stock the new Jeffrey Archer, if it looks like being a goer.

Shinto will save you a packet on furniture and crockery. You sit on a tiny mat and eat from a tiny bowl. Your wife sits behind a screen, with your other robe, and will run out with it, silently, if you spill anything from the tiny bowl. The main drawback with Shinto is that, if things don't work out, you will be expected to disembowel yourself. However, since you do not own a bookshelf, nobody will ever give you the new Jeffrey Archer.

So there you are. Bags of choice. And remember, should

you prefer to remain Christian after all but want to take no further part in the festive hokum, that the **Mormons** are always on the lookout for new recruits. They are a nice crowd, but there is one drawback: you will have to spend Christmas going from door to door in a smart blue suit with a permanent grin on your face, telling everyone you meet about this wonderful book of yours. You will thus run the constant risk of being mistaken for Jeffrey Archer.

Never Again

Oh, look at the calendar: it is National Crunch Day. It is 14 January. It is the day on which, according to a survey in last weekend's press, huge numbers of you will, after a fortnight of rug-gnawing abstention, resume smoking, boozing, eating beef on the bone, discussing Northern Ireland and leaving the lavatory seat either up or down, depending on your partner of choice.

That is because the majority of New Year resolutions, it seems, last only two weeks. But I have scant sympathy for you, since, clearly, you have yet again committed the basic error of making the wrong resolutions. I, on the other hand, made all the right ones, which I have thus been able to keep, and will, furthermore, be able to keep on keeping. I know this, because I have been keeping them for the past 30 years. That is what you have to do with resolutions: choose the right ones, for the right reasons, and stick to them, New Year in, New Year out.

In 1968, for example, I resolved not to visit Hadrian's Wall. I decided there would be little point in it, I would go all that way, look at what is left of it, express a cliché or two, and then come all that way home again. I should point out here to angry murophiles that I have made no such resolutions about the Great Wall of China. The Great Wall of China is a bit special, it is the only human artefact visible from the moon, and I am resolved to visit it some day and, from it, wave at the night sky.

I shall, however, never water-ski. That is a resolution I made even more than 30 years ago when I first saw someone doing it. It occurred to me then that if God had wanted men to be pulled on a string behind a boat, He wouldn't be much of a god. Girt as it is with unshakeable faith, this resolution has been particularly easy to keep.

Less easy has been the one made when I was 25, never to see another definitive performance of *Hedda Gabler*. It has been less easy only because there has been, if reviewers are to be believed, a definitive performance of *Hedda Gabler* every year since then, and friends phone up to ask me to go to it with them, and I am running out of excuses about washing my hair or worming the cat. I lack the bottle to tell them that it is a ropey play and no amount of definitive performances will ever alter that fact.

No difficulty at all attaches to the resolution made with greater relish, thanks to exponentially rising prices, every 1 January, because it has saved me thousands of pounds since I first hit upon it in the early 1970s. It is the determination never to bespeak a bespoke suit, but to buy only off the peg, at a fraction of the hand-made price. I prefer this because I have many friends who get suits made which cost them an arm and a leg, and you can clearly see that this is what they have done, since either one arm or one leg is shorter than the other, and not infrequently both.

I also resolved, a fortnight ago, not to keep a parrot in 1998, the twentieth time I have done this. In 1977, I did think about keeping a parrot, because writing is a lonely life, it would sit on a perch in the loft and chat to me between scribblings, but after detailed inquiries I discovered that 98 per cent of parrots never say anything, 2 per cent of parrots say the same thing over and over again, and 100 per cent of parrots bite you.

Ukuleles are, of course, a different matter, except where resolutions are concerned. Soon after I resolved not to keep a parrot, I bought a ukulele on not dissimilar, merely less psittacine, grounds, ie it would mitigate the attic solitude if I could now and again break off from the typewriter to accompany myself in a spirited rendition of *Leaning On A Lamppost*. In consequence, I spent a month so locked in digital battle with the first chord in *The George Formby Ukulele Book* that my fingers ended up literally fretted, leaving me unable not only to type without whimpering, but also to open the the door without using my elbows. 1998 is thus the twentieth year in which I am resolved not to learn the ukulele.

So there you have it. A few handy tips. And if, on 14 January 1999, I learn that you have been spotted at Hadrian's Wall with water-skis on one shoulder of an ill-cut suit and a parrot on the other, strumming your yukulele with an Ibsen ticket-stub, even the scant sympathy I expressed at the outset will disappear altogether.

Hey, Small Spender!

I have a doppelgänger. Sadly, though, I know very little about him, other than that wherever he is ganging as my doppel, he is ganging there in cheap shoes, and might also be carrying a door. Possibly a tool-kit, too. Perhaps on a bicycle. This may be somewhat tricky for him should he be drunk, especially if it is windy in Hull, because managing a bicycle while carrying a tool-kit in one hand and a door in the other is awkward enough at the best of times, but if you have just tied on a few large ones and there are gales about . . . you will, I'm sure, get the picture.

Not, mind, the whole picture. For if you have mentally gummed my face on to the bald head of the cyclist, imagined him flashing my cheesy smirk as he wobbles through the storm-tossed byways of Humberside, you must now ungum it, since my doppelgänger doesn't look like me, he is my doppelgänger only by virtue of the card in his pocket. Because when he goes into a shop to buy a door or a spanner, it is my name he signs on the slip that chatters from the till after the shopkeeper has swiped the card my doppelgänger has given him.

Good word, swiped. It allows me to segue seamlessly into the fraught explanation of all this, since in order for these assorted shopkeepers to swipe my card, it had first to be swiped by my doppelgänger. He did this (I am as sure as one can be in such matters) from the floor of a Lincoln gas station on Wednesday, that being the last time I used it, in a bit of the sort of hurry where things can get dropped: though I didn't twig this until Friday, when I opened my wallet and the card wasn't in its snug little slot. But it had, as I discovered after I rang the card company to nullify it, been, interim, through a lot of other little slots.

In Hull. Where the first thing it bought was a pair of trainers for £24.99. A puzzle, that: you can pay £100 for a good pair of trainers, so why, if it wasn't you that was paying, would you buy the worst? Pity for the true bill-footer? Hope of judicial mitigation if you ever got nicked? No good ones in your size? If so, did he have very large feet or very small ones? I wanted to know. I wanted it even more after the card-company told me the second purchase: it was a front door from the Hull B&Q. The dwarf/giant had padded round there in his new shoes, and bought a door. For £80. Odd. I've never been to Hull, but it is a serious town, it must have chic shops, it must sell Leicas, Rolexes, Armani togs; I do not wish to boast, but my credit limit would have taken care of these, so why, once committed to a course of action which hangs sheep as well as lambs, would a thief's first thought be to buy a door? A cheap door, moreover, because when I phoned B&Q, they said doors went from £56 to £249.

Then he bought a tool-kit, but he didn't buy it at B&Q, he bought it from Do-It-All; was he trying to cover his tracks? Clearly, he wanted to hang this front door of his – ours – but he didn't want B&Q to know he didn't have the tools to do it. Why? Because they might remember him, if the Old Bill ever asked, a man of 4ft 6in or 6ft 4in, in new shoes, buying not only a door but a tool-kit, too? If that was his reasoning, I wonder what he did with these purchases when he popped in to buy a bottle of Scotch? Surely the proprietor of Victoria Wine would remember a man with a door? He might even have bantered, as such chaps do, nice door you got there, nice tool-box, I wouldn't drink if I was hanging a door, mind, ha-ha-ha, tricky item, your Johnny hinge . . .

And why just one bottle? We could afford a case. Why

not a whole bicycle, either? Because that's where he went next, not to buy a whole bike, just one wheel. I suddenly felt sorry for the man who was, very briefly, me: the man who had been limping about in worse than the cheapest shoes, behind a bust front door, desperate for the drink he could not afford because he was saving up for a new wheel on a bike which was either too big for him, or too small. Do we get a fuller picture now? Is my doppelgänger not so total a loser that he has no idea what to do when he is, for once, a finder? I feel for him. I hope Hull's finest don't spot his new door, bound to have been hung upside down.

For there, but for the grace of God, gang I.

The Lavatory Will See You Now

Tell me, am I alone in feeling just a little uneasy at the thought that, any day now, our lavatories will be on the phone to our doctors? And that they will be calling up in order to reveal those literally innermost secrets which hitherto have been held in sacred trust between man and thunderbox? Did you, too, not experience, after reading this peculiar disclosure in Monday's *Times*, a faint tremor?

The source was a report by the Institution of Chemical Engineers entitled *Future Life: Engineering Solutions for the Next Generation*, keenly endorsed, as if things weren't bad enough, by the Prime Minister. I enter the caveat because I suspect not his integrity, but his attention-span: he is endorsing far too much these days, hardly an hour goes by without another 50 barmy ideas getting the full Tony, I see him sitting at his desk like some manic postal-order clerk, rubber stamp in hand, as dotty notions are shoved in front of him for a cursory glance, a lensbite smile and an imprimaturial thwack before being snatched away again and carried off to become a permanent component of the New Britain.

And the most unsettling feature of his latest endorsement is that it welcomes not merely this whistle-blowing khazi, this porcelain nark designed to analyse our ex-breakfast and transmit a pathology report direct to our GP's computer, but its envisaged successor, a microscopic biosensor planted within our very brains, able to reveal everything it learns to anyone it tells. This development, mind, is some way off, could take months, but it's wise to be prepared, so I thought I might offer you a few random thoughts while there is still time, ie, while I can still get paid for offering them; because, after my brain-chip is fitted, you'll doubtless be able to get them gratis, they will turn up on your gas bill or your fax machine, having failed to connect with my neurologist's laptop, that is how it is with computers, as you well know. Either that or I'll be dead, following my potty's misinterpretation of its waste-scan, thanks to the cat's defecatory intervention, with the result that I shall have been operated on for the removal of a hairball, and expired on the table because the faulty microchip in the surgeon's brain was following instructions from a Barclays cash dispenser.

Nor am I much happier with the less terminal side of things, having read that the biosensor can be programmed to monitor a prescribed diet, so that should it detect any signs that this is not being adhered to, it will page its host to that effect. You would, say, be sitting happily in the Savoy Grill, you would order a T-bone steak and a bottle of Beaune, and before the waiter had jotted it down, a voice from your breast-pocket would cry: 'Pay no attention, the man's a fool to himself, bring him a bit of boiled cod and a small Perrier!'

Do, furthermore, any doctors welcome all this? Has anyone asked? Is the average GP so underworked that he is currently hugging himself in anticipation of that day when all his phones are ringing all the time and the smoke is billowing from his computer as the surgery's technology struggles to handle not only genuine calls – be they from the chips of countless patients who would never them-selves have bothered him with this hot flush or that funny turn, or from hypochondriacs desperate to find out what their biosensors think they might be suffering from – but also twice as many errant cris-de-coeur from signal boxes, petrol pumps and supermarket checkouts? And will the health service ever have the resources to act upon this avalanche of diagnostic chaff?

I doubt it, just as I doubt even more our desire to be thus monitored. Hectored as we already are by the mass of medical fodder that pours from every page and channel to the point where no ailment, however recherché, however unlikely, fails to fuel our *timor mortis* – could this be why I have that tweak, that blotch, that shake, that sniff? – do we really want the already unhealthy preoccupation with our health to take a quantum leap into total obsession? Our fathers knew so little about what their bodies might be getting up to that they hardly ever thought about them, but our children might end up knowing so much as to be rendered utterly incapable of thinking about anything else.

Unbending The Rules

I was in a cheery Cape Town bar last Saturday evening, sipping a Bloody Mary and attempting to chew my complimentary wedge of biltong, a Boer titbit fashioned from old bicycle saddles, when my eye happened upon the headline of a newspaper on the seat beside mine. BOWING OUT!, it shrieked, beneath, dear God, a snapshot of HM the Queen. Palpitating, I snatched it up, fearing abdication – I had been far from civilisation for two weeks, reading nothing save menus and the odd wine-list – but though the text beneath thankfully proved to be less disastrous than that, it was bad enough. A hemisphere away, major constitutional reforms had, in my absence, been set in train: subjects would no longer be required to bow or curtsy to their sovereign. I did not hesitate. I dropped the biltong (now rehydrated to the size and consistency of a squash ball) into a waste-bin, drained my drink in a single gulp, and caught the next plane back to England.

Not as dramatic a gesture as it sounds, mind, since my flight had just been called and my only option would have been to remain in the airport bar until my snack had swollen so irremovably as to leave the airline no alternative but to bag me up and inform my next-of-kin, but still one I was glad to make; for there is no better opportunity than a 12-hour flight for someone wishing to reflect on the three occasions on which he attempted to kow-tow to his monarch, but, each time, signally failed.

My first shot was in 1978, at a party for the marriage of the Prince and Princess Michael of Kent, an event so packed that, to this day, I suspect my own invitation to have resulted merely from a desperate bid to get St James's into the *Guinness Book of Records* under the category Most People Ever Jammed Into A Royal Palace. Forewarned of Her Majesty's attendance, I had spent two weeks practising a full repertoire of obeisances ranging from slight nod to papal Tarmac-kiss, depending on circumstances. On the night, the circumstances were that, when the Queen came to bisect the throng, my face was pressed into the neck of the man in front, my own neck being held rigid by the nose behind it. I could have lifted both feet off the ground and she wouldn't have noticed.

She didn't notice my next bow either, because the dog got it. Invited to a Palace lunch, I was ushered into line, between Derek Nimmo and a tiny African bishop, to await the opening of doors through which the Queen would imminently enter. These duly parted; whereupon, though hardly tenser than a clay-pigeon trap, I instantly bowed, to a corgi that had trotted in first. Worse, when Her Majesty closely followed, I was still so mortified by the gaffe of honouring the mutt over its gracious mistress that I compounded it by failing to bow at all. The Queen of course was very decent about it, she didn't lash out or anything, but I have to tell you that she and I have not broken bread together since.

We did, however, meet a couple of years later, at Royal Ascot. I say meet: she was, in truth, hurtling down the course in her open barouche, granting the loyal punters ranged against the rails the opportunity to acknowledge their liege lady by, not bowing this time, but doffing their serried toppers as she passed, in what became, unbrokenly, a toffs' Mexican wave. Until it reached me: for when, that morning, I had collected my little grey number from Moss Bros, the fact that it was a size too small hadn't seemed important; the opposite, indeed, since it meant that no untoward gust would leave me inelegantly pursuing it across Ascot Heath, or worse, watching a thoroughbred hoof demolish my deposit. What, however, it also meant was that the hat would prove to be undoffable: I was still struggling to unscrew it with both hands as the Queen became a waving dot.

A decade has elapsed since then, but throughout it I bore my chagrin well, confident that some future moment would offer me redemption: she would unveil some plaque, launch some rugger, open some cats' home, and there my vertebrae would be, at the forefront of the mob, hingeing impeccably, at last. But now it seems this is not to be; and on Sunday, I cabbed out of Heathrow into an England that, though a spring sun shone, was unquestionably a little greyer than I had left it.

Snake In The Grass

Now that the Great Drought is at long last officially over and each and every one of us has finished clearing away the detritus of our various propitiatory rites – the high altars defestooned, the corn-dollies back in their baskets, the scrolls of the law returned to their arks, the morris-staves clipped in their racks, the prayer mats rolled up and stacked, the goats' blood sluiced from path and patio, the bells, books and candles laid lovingly away, and

Stonehenge back to normal office hours – it is time for the nation to look to its hoses.

Because, if you cast your minds back across the desiccated years, you will recall that he was always a tricky customer, your Johnny hose, and things, I promise, will only have got trickier with the long lack of use. Now, for example, is the time to cut off the split ends of dried-out hoses so that they fit snugly on to the garden tap; or would, if the jubilee clip designed to secure them had not rusted solid during the interim, thanks to the drip that was coming out of the tap before the pipe burst during the cold snap of 1990. Wisely, at the time, you turned the service off at the mains, resolved to replace it after the drought was over, though unwisely forgetting all about it until yesterday, when, turned on again, a horizontal jet filled your wellingtons to the knee.

Never mind: for the average DIY enthusiast, it is not too difficult to remove the faulty upstand pipe and tap, stanch the blood with a towel, pop down for a few simple stitches and a tetanus shot, telephone a plumber, and thus be ready, within less than a week, to secure to the new tap your neatly cut hose. Which, as the result of being neatly cut, will now be some nine inches too short to reach the one bed that requires regular watering. No matter, any nurseryman or ironmonger will be able to supply you with an extra length of hose and a connector with which you can effortlessly fail to join the new bit to the old, since the old is too thick to fit into the connector. The best remedy is to buy an entirely new hose of the required length; there is no other certain method of finding out that the new tap the plumber has just soldered onto the new upstand pipe is itself 2mm wider than the hose. This problem can be solved by opening your kitchen window and attaching the hose to your narrower kitchen tap; do bear in mind, though, that this means that the new hose will now be some nine inches too short to reach the one bed that requires regular watering.

While you're at the nursery/ironmonger, be sure to buy a new sprinkler to replace the one which has, not surprisingly, disappeared during the Great Drought. There are two main varieties of sprinkler on the market, the one that fails to spin round and the one that fails to sweep back and forth. Personally, I prefer the latter: at least you get half the garden sodden and know which side the shrubs are going to rot. The other variety sets up little oases at random, and it is all too easy, when strolling across a recently irrigated stretch, to find oneself sinking up to the shin in a little local quicksand.

While you are still at the shop, here is a handy tip. In the old days before the Great Drought, most gardeners promised themselves that one day they would jettison their old hose-reel, which was freestanding and tended to pursue them across the garden during reeling, and buy a wall-mounted reel. They may feel that day has now come, especially as it would be a way of celebrating the end of aridity; of, quite literally, splashing out. The handy tip is not to do it. This is because there is no masonry screw so secure as to hold a wall-mounted reel in permanent place: the fifth time you wind it, it will dismount and pursue you across the garden. If it is the really expensive kind, designed to reel in at the touch of the button the average DIY enthusiast has connected to the mains, it will not only pursue you, it will electrocute you first.

And that I'm afraid is just about all the useful advice I can give you about garden hoses. I do, however, have one interesting statistic to offer: Hozelock, the nation's premier supplier, tells me that some seven million homes use hoses, at an average length of 55 metres. This tots up to 240,000 miles, enough to reach to the Moon. Or, to be precise, to within nine inches of it.

Zip Code

I fear that I am, at long last, beginning to fear for President Clinton. I didn't fear before, because I had nothing to fear but fear itself, and I didn't fear it, even though others did: they feared that each new jot and tittle of salaciousness, jotted in the press, tittled on the box, would finally generate a fear in the American people that their President was unfit to preside. But I never feared that fear, and, though I do not wish to preen, the pollsters proved me right, for, as the toll of alleged peccadilloes rose, so did the President's ratings. It would seem that Americans don't care what Bill gets up to. They love him, because he's, I don't know, because he's just their Bill.

So when on Monday the latest allegation shimmied from the woodshed in the comely shape of Kathleen Willey, I thought no more about it. It wasn't until I put down the newspaper and looked out of the window that the more occurred to me; because I had suddenly spotted a small cloud on the horizon, no bigger than a man's hand. And the remarkable feature of this hand was that it wasn't doing anything: it wasn't insinuating itself around a woman's waist, it wasn't settling on a woman's knee, it wasn't stroking a woman's cheek, it wasn't even pressing an intercom button to say it didn't want to be interrupted for at least three minutes. Yes, spot on, you are there before me, that was the more – Mrs Willey had set me thinking not about all the many women Bill Clinton had possibly propositioned, but about all the far greater many he unquestionably hadn't. For it is these, I now fear, who will topple him.

I began by recalling that of all the allegations who had strutted their stuff over the past few years, none had been

Black, Hispanic, Asian, Oriental, Native American, or Inuit. Nor could I bring to mind any who were sitting in wheel-chairs, walking with guide-dogs, adjusting their hearing-aids, speaking in sign, or manifesting any other indication of being differently abled. President Clinton is not, in short, an equal opportunities philanderer; and my first fear, there-fore, is that when this unsettling observation finally perme-ates his currently supportive flock, their support will rapidly ebb. Placard-wielding minorities of every conceiv-able disposition will besiege Pennsylvania Avenue, roaring their demands for positive unzipping, before marching on to the Supreme Court to file their exotic constitutional claims, and marching out again, bound for the television studios of Oprah Winfrey and Rikki Lake and Jerry Springer, to beat the breasts which the President ignored.

Fearful enough, but I further fear he ain't heard nuthin' yet. He ain't heard from all the lawyers of all the conven-tionally-abled women he chose not to manhandle, even though they presented him with every reasonable opportu-nity. There are more than 400 of these in the White House alone, hapless dreamers who blew their savings on Versace and Chanel in order to be at their most toothsome when leaning over a photocopier, or reaching up to open a tran-som, or erranding an Oval Office doughnut, or – after lengthy research into the President's corridor schedule – gathering tactically dropped files from around his inter-rupted feet in a valiant effort at décolletage-maximisation. And, all this having proved to be of no avail, can you not envisage the consequences, as the rejected find themselves unable to hold up in public the heads they were not invited to hold down in private? How long can it be before the furi-ous scorn'd dispatch themselves sobbing to some expensive shrink, who will prescribe immediate esteem-saving resig-nation, before passing them along to his brother, the expensive attorney, who will joyously file suit against the President for constructive dismissal, grievous mental harm, and sexual non-harassment, all fees to be met, since you ask, from the proceeds of the subsequent bestselling auto-biography, blockbuster movie, television series, ice extrava-ganza, and comprehensive range of personalised oven-ware, negotiated by his son, the expensive agent?

Not long, is how long. Because the sad fact of presiden-tial life is that you can fool with some of the women some of the time, and some of the women all the time, but you cannot fool with all the women all of the time.

One Small Snip For Man

I have just washed my hair, and I can do a thing with it. I can populate the stars. All I have to decide is whether this would be a good thing to do with it. If I decide that, then my next move will be to disentangle five hairs from this wet comb, tape them to a piece of paper, and post them, along with 50 dollars, to Mr David Goldstein. He will do the rest.

It is a major rest. For Mr Goldstein is a senior banana at Encounter 2001, the Californian consortium which plans to build a spacecraft designed to carry the hairs of four-and-a-half million Earthlings – five hairs from each, at ten bucks a sprout – into the interstellar unimaginableness. How the company arrived at that curiously precise figure of 22.5 million hairs, the report does not tell us – though a shrewd guess might be that the project was costed out at 225 million dollars, that someone at the boardroom table described this as a hair-raising sum, and that a lightbulb then clicked on above Mr Goldstein's own head – but what it does tell us is what Encounter 2001 is hoping on the hairs' behalf: it is hoping not simply that they will fetch up, eventually, against some distant star, but also that this star will be populated by beings so smart as to twig that they could manufacture Earthlings by cloning them from the DNA blueprints in the hair.

Long odds, eh? Even if the spacecraft does bump into something, even if it doesn't explode into a thousand bits upon bumping, even if the bumpee is inhabited by a creature canny enough to come running at the bump, even if the runner does discover, intact, the boxful of hairs, might not there still be an outside chance (you should know that we have, so far, already reached odds of approximately a trillion squillion to one) that it will assume the hair to be no more than packing material, and rummage thoughtlessly through it in the hope of finding a carriage clock or a personal organiser, or whatever it is that intelligent beings in outer galaxies send off for, allowing 28 days for delivery? It is not, however, these remote[100] likelihoods which are currently delaying my envelope to Mr Goldstein. On the contrary, what stays my plucking finger from the comb this morning is the yet remoter one that his crackpot scenario might actually play for real: which is to say, that one fine day, however many light years off, the hairs will indeed arrive at the only star in the Milky Way prepared to do more than merely shine and twinkle, where the residents, when a rocket demolishes their birdbath and a box of hairs falls out, will cry: 'Wow! An

Earthling kit!', and immediately rush round to the local cloner's.

Because that is where my worries really begin. It is all very well for a hair to boldly go where none has gone before, but how bold might it have to be when it gets there? Not only do I not know what shape, literally, I should be in when cloned, a vulnerable baby, a spotty teenager, the middle-aged wreck sitting at this keyboard, nor who my four-and-a-half million new compatriots might turn out to be (can we doubt the presence of the raving-mad gene in the DNA of many of those prepared to fork out fifty bucks on this bizarre enterprise?), I know even less about Mr Goldstein's putative Milkians. While he is no doubt praying that his millions of potential subscribers will imagine them to be just as they themselves are – cheery Middle-American humanoids who will, while waiting for the hair to come back from the regenerator, spend their time stocking welcome-wagons, igniting barbecues and getting their bowling-balls down from the shelf – they could just as easily be Brobdingnagian fans of Subbuteo who will expect my hapless clone to spend the rest of his life running about in Crystal Palace strip, or inconceivably repugnant items of some unearthly sexual orientation who will expect even worse, or, worse even than that, slavering omnivores who have spent their lives wondering whether there was edible life in other galaxies.

So I think, on balance, not. I shall take the comb which has lain beside me on the desk as I typed, and tweak its contents into my waste-bin. Hair today and gone tomorrow, perhaps, but at least I know where.

147

Punch And Judy

O n the afternoon of 28 June 1949, my best friend David Paige came over to my house, and, it being a fine warm day, we went out into the back garden and took our shirts off, and he punched me in the stomach. I then punched him in the face. We carried on like this for a bit, until my mother opened the kitchen window and shouted that it was teatime, so David held his nose under the garden tap to stop it bleeding and I ran my finger along my teeth to make sure they could still handle a rock-cake, and we went inside and my mother put the plates and the Tizer on the table and asked if I wanted a cold flannel on my eye and I said no, and she said please yourself but you won't be able to see out of it in the morning, and she was absolutely right, God bless her, it was the best thing to happen to me that summer: hitherto, girls had never taken the slightest interest in me, but when I turned up at Osidge Primary next morning with an eye the size and colour of a King Edward potato, five of them asked me if it hurt, three begged to touch it, and Stella Cox let me walk her home.

How, you inquire, can I be so sure of the date? I can be so sure of the date because it was the day after the eleventh birthday for which my father had bought me two pairs of boxing gloves, and David Paige was naturally the first person I wanted to punch, because he was my best friend. He was not, mind, called David Paige during our brief bout, he was called Freddie Mills, and I was called Bruce Woodcock; these two idols having, just three weeks previously, knocked seven bells out of one another for the British heavyweight championship, there was nobody else we could possibly have been.

Let us come now to the only excuse for all this maudlin reminiscence, Miss Jane Couch. For she is the Women's World Welterweight Champion, but until last Monday she had been unable to fight professionally in this country because the British Boxing Board of Control had refused her a licence, on the grounds that she might be prone to harm in the ring if suffering premenstrual tension. However – though flies lucky enough to have been on the wall during these BBBC discussions will still be rolling helplessly around – events have now moved dramatically on. Miss Couch, who is not known as the Fleetwood Assassin for nothing, refused to take this defeat lying down: she sprang up from the canvas, demanded a rematch under industrial tribunal rules, and, last Monday, got the decision, on sexual discrimination points. She is keenly looking forward to her first domestic match.

But I am not. I have, I know, to tread very warily here – *The Times* has a million feisty female readers, and the Cricklewood Assassin is no longer in 1949 shape – yet how can I possibly rejoice for their new heroine when all I can think of, this morning, is the heroine-worship she is bound to inspire? Don't get me wrong, this isn't terror talking, I speak here not of the prospect of aerobics classes yielding fashionably to ringcraft ones to the point where, say, an inadvertent trolley-clash will leave me measuring my length on the Waitrose floor, unnerving though that unquestionably is, but of the far more unsettling one of what Miss Couch's triumph will mean for the nation's infant girlhood. I speak it with all the authority of someone who was, once upon a time, Bruce Woodcock.

For they are all out there waiting, the tiny wannabes. Any day now, they will wannabe Jane Couch, they will wannabe Assassins, they will wannabe Uppercut Spice and Left Jab Spice and Right Hook Spice, they will have birthdays, too, and their politically right-on daddies will not dare to resist the furious pleading. Oh sure, the daddies may attempt, initially, to fob them off with the Sugar Ray Barbies and Southpaw Sindies and My Little Flyweights which will be huckstered from the toy industry's bandwagon, but the kids will not settle for that. For the day must now inexorably come when little girls will insist on going over to their best friends' houses in order to thump them senseless.

Forgive me, female readers, call me unreconstructed, I shall just have to handle it. What I can't handle is this image I have of little Stella Cox walking home, alone, with a cauliflower ear.

Nocturnal Emissions

Lucky man, Wordsworth. When he lay upon his couch in vacant or in pensive mood, what flashed upon his inward eye were daffodils. What I get is clinics. They do not fill my heart with pleasure, they fill it with palpitations. It does not want to dance with them, it wants to get up off the couch, very carefully, and phone a cardiologist.

This will come as excellent news to the clinics. It is precisely why they paid good money to have themselves flashed upon my inward eye: in the hope that it would be the inward eye of a hypochondriac, ie, the sort of person who lies sleepless on his nocturnal couch worrying whether his eye is more inward than it was yesterday, and, if so, whether he should seek medical advice to see if anything can be done to make it more outward.

Those to whom the clinics paid the money are, of course, all the radio stations which the clinics cannily targeted at the wee small hours of the morning because that is the time when hypochondriacs are lying awake with their inward eyes flashing. There is, indeed, one clinic which nightly announces itself at 3am by asking whether you have any trouble sleeping, not unreasonably expecting you to say wow, what a terrific clinic, it is able to diagnose by radio, I wonder what service it is offering, let me listen on, good heavens, it is a sleep therapy clinic, what a coincidence, I should ring it right away, hang on, if it's any good they'll all be asleep. Never mind, I'll give them a bell first thing in the morning.

I do not object to the sleep therapy clinic, mind; it is at least offering its services at an appropriate time. I object to all the other clinics which, by offering their services at inappropriate times, rob me of the sleep the sleep therapy clinic wants to sell me. This they achieve by constantly interrupting the music I listen to in the hope it will get me to sleep. The music comes along a wire between my bedside radio and the plug in my ear, with a view to gently closing my inward eye; but too often, just as the inward lid is dropping, the music suddenly stops and a clinic bursts in to inquire whether I have noticed any of my freckles getting larger lately, at which point the inward eye snaps open and begins passing my freckles in review, an exercise which can quickly bring a hypochondriac out in so saturant a sweat that he is still sopping when, after the next three records, a new clinic comes on and wants to know if he suffers night sweats, it could be serious, ring this number.

Thus, the vacant mood you are after for a decent night's kip is doomed to turn progressively more pensive as you find yourself pondering the options of liposuction and nose-job, trying to determine whether your arches have fallen and if so where, was that wheeze bronchial, is this a pile, how far might that toenail ingrow if I do not ring the last number which offered to sort it out, could it get as far as my knee, would this produce a wonky walk, requiring osteopathy/ultrasound/acupuncture by qualified international practitioners who have been working close to London's famed Harley Street since 1989, or lead to the hernia I could apparently get fixed in half an hour, no waiting, plus free crutch home?

That's the trouble with sleepless inward eyes, at three in the morning. They roll around frantically in the inward head like marbles in a soup-plate, seeing all sorts of things they'd never see in daylight: two nights ago, a clinic came on, after Peggy Lee had all but settled me, to invite me to have all my facial hairs removed by laser so that I would never need to shave again, thereby saving ten minutes a day. I naturally began to speculate on how I might use these ten minutes, I totted them up to make a lifetime's saving of, what, two months if I live to 80, very useful, but suppose I got to 80 and wanted to grow a beard, very patriarchal, like Tolstoy with the wind blowing through his whiskers on the station platform at, oh God, where was it, am I losing my memory, should I ring the clinic that came on after Elton John and said it was essential to spot mental deterioration early, let us quote you, no obligation, no job too large or small?

As I say, lucky man, Wordsworth. Who did live to 80, thanks to that inward eye which was the bliss of solitude. Not, as now, the curse of it.

Bin There, Done That

It has recently been borne in upon me that for a man of my advanced years never to have bothered to take a close squint at the legislative particulars of his parish is as foolish as indolence gets. For, hard though it may be for you to believe, I have spent half those years in the ancient purlieu of Cricklewood without once ambling round to the Town Hall to examine the vellum scrolls on which the rights of Cricklewood citizens are inscribed. I do not even know when the inscriptions took place, or under whose aegis the scriveners toiled; some might have scribbled for Aethelred, some for Cnut, others for Harold Harefoot, all men with notoriously greedy ways and therefore much given to ceding civil concessions in return for pelf and virgins.

It could well be that, as a freeholder of Cricklewood, I am entitled to graze my goats along the verges of the A41, or claim a firkin of Maundy malmsey from Tesco's, or tether my horse to the Cricklewood Jobcentre throughout the passage of two full moons. I might, who knows, be franchised to fly my hawks in Gladstone Park or to claim droit de seigneur during the hours of daylight on the Burger King forecourt. But I do not know these things, since I have never bothered to consult the scrolls. I am a fool to myself.

Why, then, have these matters been, as I say, borne in upon me now? Because of my wheelie-bin. Every Wednesday morning, I, in common with my neighbours, comply with the recent legislation under which the Cricklewood householder is required to wheel his rubbish to the perimeter of his property to await collection. Once, we all had dustbins and the binmen came down our paths, but now we trundle to and fro in harmony, meeting halfway. And every Wednesday night, we wheel our bins back in and lock the garage door after them.

Last Wednesday night, I went out to wheel mine back and found it as heavy as when I'd wheeled it out. It had not been emptied. Kipper hung heavy in the evening air. So I left it where it was, and next morning phoned the Council Refuse Dept, who promised to consult the files and ring back. This she eventually did, to inform me that, according to the chief binman's report, 'the receptacle was found to be within the householder's curtilage, and thus beyond the collection remit of our operatives.' I told her I knew nothing of curtilages, only that my bin had been left where it had always been left. She said an inspector would call. The bin remained out on Thursday night. He must have called on Friday, because the woman I shall ever think of as the Head Refusenik rang again in the afternoon to say that the inspector's report confirmed that my bin-wheels were not on the pavement, ie, beyond my curtilage. If I rectified this, she would arrange collection on Saturday. And yes, I did ask why the inspector had not himself pushed the bin two inches so that it straddled my curtilage, and she said that pushing receptacles did not fall within an inspector's remit. So it stayed out on Friday night, too.

It was not alone in this. Also staying out on Friday night was a person who breaks into cars and runs off with their radios. I discovered this on Saturday morning when I went out through the garage to see whether the bin was now empty. What I saw was that my car was now empty. So I called the police, and the three of us stood around for a bit, considering how the thief had managed to overcome the impregnability of the front of the house and enter via the pregnable garage door at the back. The bit ended when one of the coppers asked how long the wheelie-bin had been out front. I told him. He peered at it. He informed me that it had been stood on. There was a dent. He explained to me that bins should always be brought in on collection night, so that villains couldn't stand on them to climb on to garage roofs. He glanced at his colleague, to allow something unspoken to pass between them. So I told them about councils and curtilages. They told me that it was down to householders to apprise themselves of such information. It was all up the Town Hall.

So, after 30 years, I shall. There is, after all, a 1,000-to-one chance that the thief will be caught, and it is just possible that Eadwig or Harthacnut once granted local citizenry the right to give a villain a seeing-to with a red-hot poker. You never know, in Cricklewood.

Who Cares?

I make no excuse, this morning, for returning to the scene of the crime. Indeed, I should have to make excuses if I didn't; for now that villainy has been so enthusiastically grappled to the bosom of the entertainment business that every third television programme comprises (a) two glib presenters, one with a floral tie and one with good legs, (b) three clips of monochrome CCTV featuring a man with a woolly hat and a gun/brick/jemmy, and (c) a bank of telephonists waiting for eagle-eyed viewers to blow the whistle on the star of (b), all with the sole object of cozening audiences into tuning in next week to see how everything turned out, no one in the public arena can even mention a crime without subsequently apprising his tenterhooked audience of what happened next.

A page or so back, you were all shaken to the core by my report of a serious incident in Cricklewood, when a prominent wheelie-bin left outside a top red-brick villa – because a notorious council refused to empty it – was stood on by a major criminal in order to gain access to a prime garage and steal an eminent car radio worth close to three figures. You learnt that police from as far away as Colindale were alerted, and dashed to the scene in one of their fastest vans. So what, you will have been agonising over, happened next?

A lot, and very little. For, despite what must have been a nationwide manhunt involving everything from tracker dogs and frogmen to dawn raids and DNA molecules, never mind Interpol, no trace of the criminal or his booty has so far been found. Clearly, he must have been planning his getaway for years. He will go down in the annals of Colindale nick as the Napoleon of Crime. A snapshot of the wheelie-bin, taken the following day by one of the nation's leading fingerprint experts, is probably being hung, even as I write, in Scotland Yard's Black Museum.

So far, so grim; but is there you ask, no hope, no ray of sunshine in any of this? Well, as a matter of fact there is, and quite literally, too: it is part of the logo atop a letter I have this morning received from, of all people, the mastermind's unwitting accomplice, and it depicts the sun peeping out from behind a dark cloud, above the words 'Victim Support Barnet'. Yes, the council has written to me to offer solace by visiting me on my own despoliated premises, 'to provide an opportunity for you to talk about your experience of crime. Our visitors are caring and understanding people who are trained to be aware of the effects that crime can have upon victims.'

There is a telephone number, but I have not rung it yet. I have been wondering what sort of caring, understanding person Barnet Council sends round to victims who have had their car radios pinched. An old dear with a Thermos of tea and a packet of HobNobs, perhaps, telling me how well she understands the misery of grinding round the North Circular without Jimmy Young or Jenni Murray to lighten the gloom? Some barking JP from the Viewers and Listeners Association shouting how lucky I am not to have to listen any longer to the wreckage of Radio 4 brought about by sexually deviant teenage Trotskyite controllers? A green militant from Barnet's Department of Environmental Health urging me, now that I have been lucky enough to lose one of the reasons for using private transport, and a noise-pollutant one at that, to get my entire car stolen? A coked-up kid in a souped-up Cosworth, who, as part of his caring job experience will offer to thunder me through the sleeping suburb at 3am with all windows down and all megawatts blasting, to compensate me for all the pirate hardcore techno I must be missing? A kaftanned exponent of the Barnet Technique, who will give me a free incense pot and explain how it attaches to the dashboard by a handy rubber sucker to aid that silent meditation which is so much better for my karma than John Humphrys?

Thanks, but no thanks. What this victim really wants is someone from Barnet Council to put his hands up to the responsibility for the radio's being swiped in the first place and come round here with a nice new one in a beribboned box. But I rather fear that in the matter of true care and understanding, the council and I are on different wavelengths.

All At C

We are in for a somewhat kurious time, you and I.
This morning, when I sat down in the attik to kobble
my weekly artikle, desk all kleared up ready, koffee kup at
my elbow, fresh pakket of sigarettes open beside it, I
diskovered that the letter, the one between b and d, had
seased to funktion on my komputer keyboard. I tapped it
in the normal way, the key dessended, but the letter did
not kome up on the skreen. What kame up was a blank. It
is probably just a bit of mukk under the key, I thought. It
is making it stikk. All I have to do is unskrew the kasing,
blow the mukk off, give everything a quikk wipe-over
with a piese of kotton-wool soaked in surgikal spirit,
replase the kasing, and Bob's your unkle. But when I
unskrewed it, I diskovered that Bob was not my unkle at
all. There was no mukk in there. Everything was as klean
as a whistle.

So I skrewed the kasing bakk on, and I konsulted the
handy stikker on the back of my komputer, and I telephoned the Apple Makintosh helpline, and a young jap
said: 'Peter speaking, how may I help you?' And I told Peter
my problem and Peter said that this was a fairly kommon
okkurrense, though it was usually an e, bekause e was the
letter that did most work, did I know that, and I said yes I
did, but in my kase it seems to be a see, kan it be repaired,
and Peter said no problem, and he gave me the name of my
nearest Apple repair sentre.

So I thanked him, and I diskonnekted the keyboard and
went downstairs with it, kursing a bit bekause I did not
want to be driving my kar to Edgware this morning. I
wanted to be kobbling my artikle in Krikklewood, and

158

when I got to Edgware I found myself kursing even more, bekause there was a long queue of other people kursing, also waving various bits of Makintosh at the man behind the kounter, who set all our minds at rest by telling us he had only one pair of hands; but after about an hour or so those hands were finally on my keyboard, and he unskrewed it and poked about in it, and he said, 'Yes, the see has definitely pakked up,' and I said, 'Kan you fit a new see?' and he said, 'It wouldn't be worth it, it would kost you 30 quid labour and before you knew it another letter would pakk up, this is an old keyboard, you're better off buying a new one, it would pay in the long run,' and I said, 'All right, fine, kould you let me have one, then?' and he said, 'No kan do, I'm afraid, this is an obsolete model, we do not karry obsolete stokk, best I kan do is order you one from Sentral Wossname,' and I said 'How long would that take?' and he said 'How long is a piese of string, might get it by next week, kan't promise,' and I said 'Next week, next week, what good is that, I have a deadline tonight,' and he said 'Well, you'll have to do it longhand, then,' and I said, 'How kan I do it longhand, I have to do it on a komputer, my komputer is konnekted to a modem, I tap the words out on it and I press a button and the stuff goes into the telephone and straight into page at *The Times* a few sekonds later, you kannot do that with a bit of paper with squiggles all over it, we are living in the Twentieth Sentury.' And he said, 'Sorry life's a bitj, innit, do you want me to order up a new keyboard, or what?' and I told him yes, and I turned away to go off to find a sekluded spot where I kould put a Luger to my temple, but as I did so a man behind in the queue, who was klutching a VDU to his jest, said, 'I kouldn't help overhearing your konversation, I hope you don't mind my putting my two penn'orth in, but I had your problem onse and I may be able to help, espesially as it is a see that has

159

gone on the fritz,' and I said, 'What do you mean?' and he said, 'Well, with a see, you kan use a k when it's hard, and an s when it's soft, it won't be diffikult for people to work it out, they must be a bright lot, *Times* readers,' and I said, 'That is a terrifik idea, thank you very muj, but what do I do when it is a kompound, you know, see and h?' and he said, 'You use a j.'

So I thanked him again, and I drove home to Krikklewood, and I went bakk up into the attik; where it suddenly struck me that I kouldn't write the artikle I originally intended to write, bekause you wouldn't know why it looked so pekuliar. I kould write only this one.

The Green Green Grass
Of Home

Were you to come out of my front gate, turn right, and walk 50 yards, you would find yourself at the A41. Were you then to turn left, and carry on walking, you would find yourself, after a bit, at the River Mersey. For the A41 is a serious road; it is a dual carriageway built to bear three broad lanes of carriages on either side, and it connects Cricklewood to Birkenhead.

You would not, of course, be walking along the carriageway, you would be walking along the pavement beside it, which is separated from the carriageway by a grass verge. You would thus be having a terrific time, but, suddenly, the terrific time would come to an end, because the grass verge does not go all the way to Birkenhead; it stops, after a mile or so, in the middle of Hendon, which means that, from Hendon to Birkenhead, the A41 ceases to be of any interest at all to the serious hiker. There is nothing worth looking at any more. He might as well be driving.

But, for that all-too-brief mile or so, everything is worth looking at. The grass verge is a treasure trove. It has so much in it that you cannot see the grass. It is nothing more nor less than a continuous ribbon of contemporary social history. Hike slowly along it with your wits and your rubber gloves about you, and by the time you get to the middle of Hendon, you will have a comprehensive portrait of our times. Thanks to the benevolent jetsam of a million carriages, to say nothing of the generous donations of not a few caring pedestrians, too, this narrow museum displays examples of everything we eat, everything we eat it out of, every bottle and can of everything we drink, every empty packet of everything we smoke, every newspaper or magazine we read, and everything for the weekend. There are gloves and batteries of every size and plastic forks and filler caps and shoes and string and spark-plugs, there are bits of toy and sunglass and umbrella and syringe and tool. There is, in short, a mile or so of all we have and are.

More yet: I, who have lived here half my life, can remember seeing all we had and were. Occasionally, kind readers write to ask me how it is that I have so rich a memory of the names of vanished beers and defunct confectionery and antique underwear and long-lost children's games and tobaccos dead and gone, I could surely not have tried them all? And they are right, I have not, but I have seen them all, down the long arches of the years, in that fecund verge.

Except on the one day in all those 30 years when there was nothing there at all. Not only was there not one single piece of – oh, all right, rubbish – on the grass, the grass itself has been cropped and edged and rolled and weeded to a standard fit to allow bowls to be played from Cricklewood to Hendon. I cannot tell you how it was done, or who did it, but when I reveal that the day was September 7, 1997, you will at least know why. For that was of course the day when the hearse carrying Diana, Princess of Wales, on its journey from Westminster, turned from Finchley Road on to the A41, to go from Cricklewood to Hendon, and on to Althorp. I stood there as she passed, a billion transglobal viewers with me, and though none of them may have been as staggered as I not to see it, none saw even a toffee-paper.

Why am I recalling this today? Because Gordon Brown needs my help. What he does not need is the maelstrom sucking at his boots, thanks to the row over the Diana Memorial Garden proposed for Kensington Palace, about which the local residents are going spare. Well, Chancellor, I think I speak for the local residents of Cricklewood when I say that the solution lies with something literally going spare, here on our doorstep; or, at least, 50 yards from it.

What I propose is the Diana Memorial Verge, a strip of England to be kept forever green and pleasant in her memory at a fraction of the cost of knocking Kensington about and thrombosing Central London's traffic, which would allow millions of pilgrims to share her final journey without even getting out of their cars and charabancs. All I ask in return is a big (but dignified) sign at the corner of Finchley Road and the A41, declaring that anyone throwing anything out of those cars and charabancs will be shot.

Jug Addiction

In the high and far-off times, Best Beloved, you decided, one morning, to pop down to the local kitchen shop and buy a coffee-machine, to provide you with fresh piping-hot coffee whenever you fancied it. The machine consisted of a plastic body which opened at the top, so that you could fill its filter with ground beans and pour water into the receptacle beside the filter, and a big glass jug which slotted into the body between the filter and hotplate, so that when the heating element in the body had done its work, the water would bubble from the receptacle, through the ground beans, and drip into the jug from which you would then pour fresh piping-hot coffee whenever you fancied. You paid only £27.95 for all this, and even got a year's guarantee thrown in.

A day or two over a year later, you fancied a cup of piping-hot coffee, switched on the machine, and returned five minutes later to find that the machine had not fancied making it. So you emptied the water out of it, and popped down to the local kitchen shop, and the shop nodded and said, yes, they'll do that, it is the element, and you said what would it cost to fix it now that it is out of guarantee, and the shop sucked its teeth and scratched its head with its pencil and muttered to itself about parts and labour and postage and packing, for all the world as if it were making genuine calculations, and finally told you it would be £25. So you said that you might as well buy a brand-new one, and the shop said what a very good idea that was, you had made the right decision there, all right, and you went home with both the old one and the new one, thinking, I've got a new coffee-machine for £2.95, and I've still got the big jug and the plug from the old one, do I know how to strike a bargain, or do I not?

At home, you cut the plug off the flex and put it in a cigar box under the stairs for future use, and you put the old jug in a kitchen cupboard, and you plugged in your new coffee-machine, and you were happy as Larry, for a year and a couple of days. And so it went on, Best Beloved, for some ten years and a dozen or so days, at the end of which you had a new coffee-machine and a cupboard with nine jugs in it, not to mention nine plugs under the stairs, neither of which collection you would ever need, because every new machine you bought came with its own jug, and every other electrical good you bought came with a plug already on it.

Why, today, have you still not thrown the old jugs away? You cannot do this, they are perfectly good jugs, even if, for ten years, you have been unable to think of anything they would be perfectly good for; you cannot put flowers in them, you cannot serve wine from them, they have calibrated sides, everybody knows they are old coffee jugs, how could they not know, they have dozens at home themselves. If you were an artist, you might string the ten jugs from a wonky rake, at different heights, call it Micronesia 14 With Uncle Jeff, and collar the Turner Prize, but that is about the top and bottom of what you can do with old coffee jugs.

Until – you guessed? – now. For I have been thinking about your problem, Best Beloved, and it has come to me that since we patently do not have nearly enough television game shows for our intellectual good, it is time to launch *Big Jugs*. First, a nationwide campaign would invite viewers to send in their surplus coffee jugs and three-pin plugs, for each of which the television company would, of course, donate one pound to charity; then, when enough jugs and plugs had been stockpiled, a cheery host appointed, and a catchy signature tune composed, the game would be launched upon a nation trebly grateful that its detritus had not only gone to both a worthy and a watchable cause, but also that it had at last freed up a useful cupboard and a handy cigar-box.

The game? Each night, at prime time, the camera would reveal three teetering pyramids of old coffee jugs, and three beloved celebrities standing at three tables piled high with three-pin plugs. The cheery host would bang a gong, and the celebrities would begin chucking the plugs at the jugs. The winner would be the celebrity who had broken most jugs with least plugs, and thus won a brand-new coffee-machine.

Seems Like Old Times

Atop a gunmetal filing cabinet, in a corner of my attic sweatshop, sits a fez. It has sat there for more than a decade now, ever since it was brought back by my daughter from a school trip to somewhere fezzy, Morocco I think, where it had suddenly come upon her that the Tommy Cooper impressions I was then wont to do at the drop of a hat might be given some semblance of credibility if I had the right hat to drop. Sadly – though only, at a guess, for me – she proved to be so mistaken in this that I gave up doing

Tommy Cooper impressions altogether, and put the fez on top of the filing cabinet, whence it has never since budged.

A pity, that, because it is a fine fez, red felt, silk-lined, black-tasselled, so born to be worn that hardly a day in the past dozen years has gone by without my gazing at it and wondering whether there would ever be an occasion when I might be called upon to wear it.

And, do you know, I rather believe that that occasion is about to come? As to the date of its coming, there is no about about it, it is a very big date indeed, it is as big a date as any of us will ever see; it is none other than 1 January 2000, that's how big a date it is. But – since I hear the crack of readers' flexing knees as they prepare to leap to conclusions – the answer is no, I shall not be sporting the fez at some tacky fancy-dress thrash, I do not plan to usher in the millennium as a bad Tommy Cooper or a worse King Farouk, I shall be wearing it up here in the loft, and I shall be wearing it as me.

Because I want my computer to be happy. What else would I want for something which wants me to be happy, too? I know it wants this from its behaviour every morning, when, solitary in the big empty house, I trudge up to the attic beneath the weight of glum infertility, plonk down before it, and flick its switch. Whereupon it plays a merry little jig, throws Mr Smiley's face upon its screen, and bids me welcome. It wants me to feel good. It wants to assure me that I am not alone. It wants me to know I have a buddy, there to share my burden; it will help me out, it will find words for me, correct errors, transpose sentences, check references, set paragraphs, count lines, number pages, and, when we are both content with what we have jointly cobbled, it will print our stuff out while I relax, light a fag, and sip my coffee. We are a team.

You will thus understand why I should be so worried

whether we will still be a team on 1 January 2000. For, a little earlier this morning, a man on Radio 4 interrupted my shaving with a remark that froze the very foam to my cheek: invited to explain the millennium bug, the man replied: 'Put simply, it means that on 1 January 2000, computers will think it is 1 January 1900.'

I sluiced off, stricken, towelled as in a trance, ran up here to the loft, and looked at my buddy, fraught with imponderability over what would happen when, on that all-too-imminent date, I switched it on. It would wonder, for a nano-second, where it was, and then, erroneously, twig. It would think it was a member of an empire on which the sun never set, it would rejoice in the goodness of God, the gentleness of women, the chivalry of men, the probity of government, the imperishability of monarchy, the sanctity of marriage. Unashamedly patriotic to its core, it would believe its countryside the greenest, its waters the purest, its sportsmen the fairest, its newspapers the truest . . .

And what would it expect of me? It would expect a Victorian man of letters. Not, that is, a dishevelled hack in track-suit and trainers, dog-end bobbing as he curses at his melamine worktop to the bong of his iffy radiator, but an impeccable dandy, in goffered mutton-chops and waxed moustache, lolling elegantly at his inlaid escritoire and drawing on a hand-rolled Burmese stogey while the Irish wolfhound by his roaring fire gazes devotedly upon this exquisite figure in the quilted velvet smoking jacket, the lace-cuffed chemise, the brocade pantaloons, the silken hose beneath the Turkish slippers. And, de rigueur, the fez.

Well, I cannot do the rest, come Millennium Day, but I can at least do the fez. It may offer my buddy a brief moment of reassurance, before I begin to drag it, kicking and screaming, into the 21st century.